First of all I wo

to thank you for purchasing this book set. Anyone, who is interested in learning Python Programming Language, These books is a great guide for beginners in python programming. This box set contains 2 books – Python Programming Book For Beginners and Complete Python Programming Guide (Second and Advanced series of 1st book). I am sure you will learn a lot from it and will become an expert in programming.

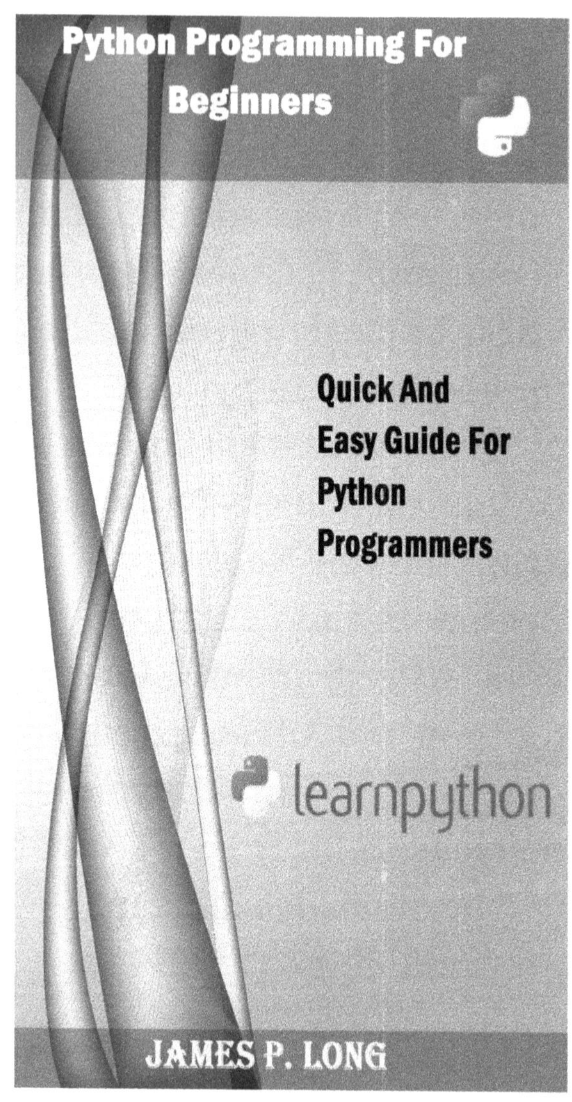
Python Programming For
Beginners
Quick And
Easy Guide For
Python
Programmers
learnpython
JAMES P. LONG

Python Programming For Beginners

Quick And Easy Guide For Python Programmers

By:

James P. Long

This publication is designed to provide accurate and authoritative information in regard to the subject matter covered. It is sold with the understanding that the publisher is not engaged in rendering legal, accounting or other professional services. If legal advice or other professional assistance is required, the services of a competent professional person should be sought.

- From a Declaration of Principles jointly adopted by a Committee of the American Bar Association and a Committee of Publishers and Associations.

ACKNOWLEDGMENTS

For my students and friends, who all selflessly helped me in writing this book. Special thanks to those who asked, insisted and assisted me in turning the seminars in this practical form.

TABLE OF CONTENTS

INTRODUCTION

WHAT IS PYTHON PROGRAMMING?

Python is a wide used general, high-level programming language. Its style philosophy emphasizes code readability, and its syntax allows programmers to precise ideas in fewer lines of code that might be possible in languages like C++ or Java. The language provides constructs supposed to modify clear programs on both small and large scales.

Python is a simple to learn, powerful programming language. Its economical high-level information structures, and an easy, but effective approach to object-oriented programming. Python's elegant syntax and dynamic typing, in conjunction with its interpreted nature, make it a perfect language for scripting and speedy application development in several areas on most platforms. Python is one in all those rare languages which might claim to both easy and powerful. You may end up pleasantly stunned to examine how easy it's to think about the answer to the matter instead of the syntax and structure of the language you are programming in.

Python supports multiple programming paradigms, as well as object-oriented, imperative and useful programming or procedural designs. It features a dynamic type system and automatic memory management and contains a giant and a comprehensive customary library.

Python interpreters are available for installation on several operational systems, allowing Python code execution on a majority of systems. Using third-party tools, like Py2exe or Pyinstaller, Python code will be packaged into complete workable programs for a few of the most fashionable operational systems, letting the distribution of Python-based software system to use in those environments without requiring the installation of a Python interpreter.

Python is a programming language that's freely available. It will be written once and run on nearly any PC with no need to alter the program. In this book, you can learn a lot about what Python is, how it's used, and the way it compares to other programming languages.

HISTORY

Python was first created by Guido van Rossum in 1990 and was named when the Brit-come Monty Python's Flying Circus. It's since been developed by an oversized team of volunteers and is freely available from the Python software system Foundation.

Python is currently found in several incarnations. At the website of the Python software system Foundation, Python is written in C, other incarnations also exist. A Java-based version of Python exists in Jython and should be used to work with Java code natively. Iron Python, a C# version, exists for the.Net and Mono platforms and allows C# programmers access to Python's power and flexibility. In each of those instances, Python is written in one language and works natively therewith language; but, it also interacts with other languages through its several modules.

For functions of analysis and development, there's also a Python implementation written in Python itself. The project PyPy was based in 2003 to modify Python programmers to alter the behavior of the Python interpreter at can. Whereas it's an open source project, being developed overtly by a community of developers for gratis distribution and modification, PyPy is also supported by the European Union as a Specified Targeted Research Project (STReP), part of the FP6 funding program.

Python is so an exciting and powerful language. It's the proper combination of performance and features that make writing programs in Python both fun and simple.

WHY IS PYTHON USED?

Python is a general purpose programming language that's ready to be used on any laptop OS. It's simply going to be used for processing text, numbers, images, scientific knowledge, or anything that one may save for a laptop. It's used daily in the operations of the Google search engine, the video sharing computing machine YouTube, NASA, and also the New York securities market. These are however many of the places where Python plays vital roles in the success of business, government, and non-profit organizations; there are several others.

In the days glided by, this sort of language was known as a scripting language, intimating its use for trivial or banal tasks. However, programming languages like Python have forced an amendment therein word. More and more, giant applications are written nearly only in Python.

Python is dynamically written, it means you don't declare a type (e.g. 'integer') for a variable name, and then assign something of that type. Instead, you have variable names, and you bind them to entities whose type stay with the entity itself. A = 5 makes the variable name 'a' to check with the whole number 5. Later, a = "hello" makes the variable name 'a' to check with a string containing "hello". Static has written languages would have you ever declare into a = 5, however, assignment a = "hello" would a compile time error.

Python is strongly written, It means if a = "5" can stay a string, and ne'er coerced to variation if the context needs therefore. Each type conversion in python should be done expressly. This can be completely different from, for instance, Perl or JavaScript, where you have weak typing, and may write things like "hello" + 5 to urge "hello5".

Python is object oriented, with class-based inheritance. Everything is an object, in the sense that they will be passed around as arguments, have strategies and attributes, and so on. Python is multipurpose; it's not specialized to a selected target of users. It's extended through modules and libraries that hook terribly simply in the C programming language.

Python enforces correct indentation of the code by making the indentation a part of the syntax. There are not any management braces in Python. Blocks of code are known of the extent of indentation. Though an enormous shut down for several programmers not used to this, it's precious because it provides an awfully uniform vague and leads to code that's visually pleasant to scan. The code is compiled into computer memory unit code, then dead during a virtual machine. This suggests that precompiled code is transportable between platforms.

Python is used for any programming task, from interface programming to internet programming with everything else in between. It's quite economical; the maximum amount of its activity is finished at the C level. Python is simply a layer on prime of C language.

FEATURES OF PYTHON

Python is a multi-paradigm programming language: object-oriented programming and structured programming are totally supported, and there are a variety of language features that support useful programming and aspect-oriented programming. Several other paradigms are supported using extensions, as well as style by contract and logic programming.

Python uses dynamic typing and a mixture of reference enumeration and a cycle-detecting refuse collector for memory management. A vital feature of Python is dynamic name resolution that binds method and variable names throughout program execution.

Python is a clear and powerful object-oriented programming language, reminiscent of Perl, Ruby, Scheme, or Java.

Python's Notable Features:

- Uses a chic syntax, making the programs you write easier to browse.

- Is an easy-to-use language that produces it easy to get your program working? This makes Python ideal for epitome development and other ad-hoc programming tasks, without compromising maintainability.

- Comes with an oversized custom library that supports several common programming tasks like connecting to net servers, looking text with regular expressions, reading and modifying files.

- Python's interactive mode makes it easy to check short snippets of code. There is also a bundled development surroundings referred to as IDLE.

- Is well extended by adding new modules enforced in a much compiled language like C or C++.

- Also can be embedded into an application to produce a programmable interface.

- Runs on many various computers and operational systems: Windows, MacOS, several brands of working systematically, OS/2.

- Is a free software system in 2 senses? It does not value something to transfer or use Python, or to incorporate it in your application. Python also can be freely changed and re-distributed; as a result of whereas the language is proprietary it's available under an open source license.

Programming-Language Features of Python Are:

- A spread of basic information sorts is available: numbers (floating purpose, complex, and unlimited-length long integers), strings (both software and Unicode), lists, and dictionaries.

- Python supports object-oriented programming with categories and multiple inheritances.

- Code will be sorted into modules and packages.

- The language supports raising and catching exceptions, leading to cleaner error handling. Information is sorted are powerfully and dynamically typewritten. - Mixture incompatible sorts (e.g. trying to feature a string and a number) causes an exception to ask, so errors are caught sooner.

- Python contains advanced programming features like generators and list comprehensions.

- Python's automatic memory management frees you from having to manually apportion and free memory in your code.

INSTALLING PYTHON TO SYSTEM

Installing Python On Your System

There are basically 2 versions of python available - Python 2 and Python 3. Look how to install python on your pc's or laptop's.

Overview of Requirements

The installation will depend on your operating system, but overall, you will need:

- Python 2.x – there are plans to update/include Python 3.x

- GIT

- A C compiler

- PIP

- Virtualenv

- Virtualenvwrapper

Installation on Windows

Visit https://www.python.org/downloads/ and download the latest version. The installation is just like any other Windows-based software.

DOS Prompt

If you want to be able to use Python from the Windows command line, i.e. the DOS prompt, and then you need to set the PATH variable appropriately.

For Windows 2000, XP, 2003

Click on Control Panel → System → Advanced → Environment Variables. Click on the variable named PATH in the System Variables section, then select Edit and add ;C:\Python27 (please verify that this folder exists, it will be different for newer versions of Python) to the end of what is already there. Of course, use the appropriate directory name.

For older versions of Windows

Open the file C:\AUTOEXEC.BAT and add the line PATH=%PATH%;C:\Python33 and restart the system. For Windows NT, use the AUTOEXEC.NT file.

For Windows Vista:

- Click Start and choose Control Panel

- Click System, on the right, you'll see "View basic information about your computer"

- On the left is a list of tasks, the last of which is Advanced system settings. Click that.

- The Advanced tab of the System Properties dialog box is shown. Click the Environment Variables button on the bottom right.

- In the lower box titled System Variables scroll down to Path and click the Edit button.

- Change your path as need be.

- Restart your system. Vista didn't pick up the system path environment variable change until you restart it.

For Windows 7 and 8:

- Right click on Computer from your desktop and select Properties or click Start and choose Control Panel → System and Security → System. Click on Advanced system settings on the left and then click on the advanced tab. At the bottom, click on Environment Variables and under System variables, look for the PATH variable, select and then press Edit.

- Go to the end of the line under Variable value and append; C:\Python27 (please verify that this folder exists, it will be different for newer versions of Python) to the end of what is already there. Of course, use the appropriate folder name.

- If the value was %SystemRoot%\system32; It will now become %SystemRoot%\system32;C:\Python27

- Click OK and you are done. No restart is required, however you may have to close and reopen the command line.

Running Python prompt on Windows

For Windows users, you can run the interpreter in the command line if you have set the PATH variable appropriately.

To open the terminal in Windows, click the start button and click Run. In the dialog box, type cmd and press enter key.

Then, type python and ensure there are no errors.

Installation on Mac OS X

For Mac OS X users, Python must be installed already.

To verify, open the terminal by pressing Command+Space keys (to open Spotlight search), type Terminal and press enter key. Now, run python and ensure there are no errors.

Installation on GNU/Linux

For GNU/Linux users, Python must be installed already.

To verify, open the terminal by opening the Terminal application or by pressing Alt+F2 and entering gnome-terminal. If that doesn't work, please refer the documentation of your particular GNU/Linux distribution. Now, run python and ensure there are no errors.

You can see the version of Python on the screen by running:

Python 2.7.6

This is all about how to successfully install Python on your System.

WRITING PROGRAMS IN PYTHON

The Python language has so many similarities to Perl, C and Java, but definitely there are some differences between the languages. In this chapter you will learn about how to write a simple program in Python. We will write, 'Hello World' program in Python. I will teach you how to write, save and run Python programs. There are two ways of using Python to run your program - using the interactive interpreter prompt or using a source file. We will now see how to use both of these methods.

- Interactive Mode Programming

- Script Mode Programming

Interactive Mode Programming

Invoking the interpreter without passing a script file as a parameter brings up the following prompt:

```
$ python

Python 2.4.3 (#1, Nov 11 2010, 13:34:43)

[GCC 4.1.2 20080704 (Red Hat 4.1.2-48)] on linux2

Type "help", "copyright", "credits" or "license" for more information.

>>>
```

Type the following text to the right of the Python prompt and press the Enter key:

```
>>> print "Hello, Python!";
```

If you are running a new version of Python, then you would need to use the print statement with parenthesis, like print ("Hello, Python!");. However, at Python version 2.4.3, this will produce following result:

```
Hello, Python!
```

If you see output like this, it means you have successfully run your python program.

Script Mode Programming

Invoking the interpreter with a script parameter begins execution of the script and continues until the script is finished. When the script is finished, the interpreter is no longer active. Let's write a simple Python program in a script. All python files will have extension .py. So put the following source code in a test.py file.

```
print "Hello, Python!";
```

Here, I assumed that you have a Python interpreter set in the PATH variable. Now, try to run this program as follows:

```
$ python test.py
```

Output:

```
Hello, Python!
```

Let's try another way to execute a Python script. Below is the modified test.py file:

```
#!/usr/bin/python

print "Hello, Python!";
```

Here, I assumed that you have Python interpreter available in /usr/bin directory. Now, try to run this program as follows:

```
$ chmod +x test.py    # This is to make file executable

$./test.py
```

Output:

```
Hello, Python!
```

If in case you got any error, then type the above program as it is and run the program again. Keep in mind that Python is case-sensitive, i.e. print is not the same as Print - note the lowercase up in the former and the uppercase P in the latter. Also, ensure that there are no spaces or tabs before the first character in each line.

BASICS OF PYTHON

PYTHON IDENTIFIERS

A Python identifier is used to identify a variable, function, class, module or other object. An identifier starts with a letter A to Z or a to z or an underscore (_) followed by zero or more letters, underscores and digits (0 to 9). Python does not allow punctuation characters such as @, $ and % within identifiers. Python is a case sensitive programming language.

Here are following identifier naming convention for Python:

- Class names start with an uppercase letter and all other identifiers with a lowercase letter.

- Starting an identifier with a single leading underscore indicates by convention that the identifier is meant to be private.
- Starting an identifier with two leading underscores indicates a strongly private identifier.
- If the identifier also ends with two trailing underscores, the identifier is a language-defined special name.

Reserved Words

The reserved words that are not used as constant or variable or any other identifier names in Python are s follows. All the Python keywords contain lowercase letters only.

And	exec	not
Assert	finally	or
Break	for	pass
Class	from	print
Continue	global	raise
Def	if	return
Del	import	try
Elif	in	while
Else	is	with
Except	lambda	yield

LINES AND INDENTATION

One of the facts to consider when learning python are that there are no braces to indicate blocks of code for class and function definitions or flow control. Blocks of code are denoted by line indentation, which is rigidly enforced. The number of spaces in the indentation is variable, but all statements within the block must be indented the same amount.

For example,

```
if True:
   print "True"
else:
  print "False"
```

However, the second block in this example will generate an error:

```
if True:
   print "Answer"
   print "True"
else:
   print "Answer"
  print "False"
```

Thus, in Python all the continuous lines indented with a similar number of spaces would form a block.

COMMENTS

Comments are any text to the right of the # symbol and is mainly useful as notes for the reader of the program. For example:

```
print 'hello world' # Note that print is a statement
```

or:

```
# Note that print is a statement
print 'hello world'
```

You can comment multiple lines as follows:

```
# This is a comment.

# This is a comment, too.

# This is a comment, too.

# I said that already.
```

You can Use as many useful comments as you can in your program to explain assumptions, explain important decisions, explain important details, explain the problems you're trying to solve and explain problems you're trying to overcome in your program, etc.

LITERAL CONSTANTS

You can use literal constants in python. The literal constants are numbers like 5, 1.23, or a string like 'This is a string' or "It's a string!".

It is called a literal because it is literal; you use its value literally. The number 2 always represents itself and nothing else; it is a constant because its value cannot be changed. Hence, all these are referred to as literal constants.

MULTI-LINE STATEMENTS

Statements in Python typically end with a new line. Python allows the use of line continuation character (\) to denote that the line should continue.

For example:

```
total = item_one + \
    item_two + \
    item_three
```

Statements contained within the [], {} or () brackets do not need to use the line continuation character.

For example:

```
days = ['Monday', 'Tuesday', 'Wednesday',
    'Thursday', 'Friday']
```

QUOTATION IN PYTHON

Python accepts single ('), double (") and triple (''' or """) quotes to denote string literals, as long as the same type of quote starts and ends the string.

The triple quotes can be used to span the string across multiple lines. For example, all the following are legal:

```
word = 'word'

sentence = "This is a sentence."

paragraph = """This is a paragraph. It is
```

made up of multiple lines and
sentences."""

COMMAND LINE ARGUMENTS

You may have seen, for instance, that many programs can be run so that they provide you with some basic information about how they should be run. Python enables you to do this with -h:

```
$ python -h

usage: python [option] ... [-c cmd | -m mod
| file | -] [arg] ...
```

Options and arguments (and corresponding environment variables):

-c cmd : program passed in as string (terminates option list)

-d : debug output from parser (also PYTHONDEBUG=x)

-E : ignore environment variables (such as PYTHONPATH)

-h : print this help message and exit

OBJECTS AND CLASSES

A class can have methods, i.e. functions defined for use with respect to that class only. You can use these pieces of functionality only when you have an object of that class. For example, Python provides an append method for the list class which allows you to add an item to the end of the list. A class can also have fields which are nothing but variables defined for use with respect to that class only. You can use these variables/names only when you have an object of that class. Fields are also accessed by the dotted notation, for example, mylist.field.

Example (save as ds_using_list.py):

```
# This is my shopping list

shoplist = ['nailpaint', 'eyeliner',
'facewash', 'lipstick']

print 'I have', len(shoplist), 'items to
purchase.'

print 'These items are:',

for item in shoplist:

   print item,

print '\nI also wnat to purchase a
perfume.'

shoplist.append('perfume')

print 'Now my shopping list is', shoplist
```

```
print 'I will sort my list now'

shoplist.sort()

print 'Sorted shopping list is', shoplist

print 'The first item I will buy is', shoplist[0]

olditem = shoplist[0]

del shoplist[0]

print 'I bought the', olditem

print 'Now my shopping list is', shoplist
```

Output:

```
$ python ds_using_list.py

My Shopping Items

These items are: nailpaint eyeliner facewash lipstick

I also want to purchase a perfume.
```

Now my shopping list is ['nailpaint', 'eyeliner', 'facewash', 'lipstick', 'perfume']

I will sort my list now

Sorted shopping list is ['nailpaint', 'lipstick', 'facewash', 'eyeliner', 'perfume']

The first item I will buy is nailpaint

I bought the nailpaint

Now my shopping list is ['lipstick', 'facewash', 'eyeliner', 'perfume']

VARIABLES TYPE

Based on the data type of a variable, the interpreter allocates memory and decides what can be stored in the reserved memory. Therefore, by assigning different data types to variables, you can store integers, decimals or characters in these variables. Python variables do not have to be explicitly declared to reserve memory space. The declaration happens automatically when you assign a value to a variable. The equal sign (=) is used to assign values to variables.

The operand to the left of the = operator is the name of the variable and the operand to the right of the = operator is the value stored in the variable.

Example:

```
#!/usr/bin/python

counter = 10          # An integer
assignment

miles   = 100.0       # A floating point

name    = "Sam"       # A string

print counter

print miles

print name
```

Output:

10

100.0

Sam

PYTHON DATA TYPES

Python has a great set of useful data types. Python's data types are built on the core of the language. They are easy to use and straight forward.

BOOLEAN VALUES

Python programming language, the Boolean data type is a primitive datatype having one of two values: True or False. This is a fundamental data type.

Example:

Peter's parents are waiting a child to be born. They have chosen a name for both possibilities. If it is going to be a boy, they will name him Thomas. If it is going to be a girl, they will name her Amby.

```
#!/usr/bin/python
# kid.py
import random
male = False
male = bool(random.randint(0, 1))
if (male):
  print "We will use name Thomas"
else:
  print "We will use name Amby"
```

The script uses a random integer generator to simulate our case.

```
import random
```

Here we import the random module that is used to calculate random numbers.

```
male = bool(random.randint(0, 1))
```

Here we use two functions. The randint() function returns a random number from the given integer boundaries. In our case 0 or 1. The bool() function converts the integers to Boolean values.

```
if (male):
  print "We will use name Thomas"
else:
  print "We will use name Amby"
```

We print the name. The if command works with boolean values. If the male is True, we print the "We will use name Thomas" to the console. If it has a False value, we print the other string.

NUMBERS

In Python programming language, we have integer numbers, floating point numbers, and complex numbers.

Example:

To count oranges.

```
#!/usr/bin/python

# oranges.py

# number of baskets

baskets = 20

# number of oranges in a basket
```

```
oranges_in_basket = 65

# we get the total number of oranges

total = baskets * oranges_in_basket

print "There are total of", total, "oranges"
```

In our script, we count the total amount of oranges. We use the multiplication operation.

Output:

```
$ ./oranges.py

There are total of 1300 oranges
```

Floating point numbers represent real numbers in computing. Real numbers measure continuous quantities. Let's say a sprinter for 100m ran 9.87s. What is his speed in km/h?

```
#!/usr/bin/python

# sprinter.py

# 100m is 0.1 km

distance = 0.1

# 9.87s is 9.87/60*60 h

time = 9.87 / 3600

speed = distance / time

print "The average speed of" \

    " a sprinter is " , speed, "km/h"
```

To get the speed, we divide the distance by the time.

```
print "The average speed of" \

    " a sprinter is " , speed, "km/h"
```

The \ character is called an escape character. The escape character changes the meaning of the new line character. We see the code in two lines, but the interpreter drops the new line character, and sees only one line. Without the escape character, the interpreter would complain about indentation.

Output:

```
$ ./sprinter.py

The average speed of a sprinter is
36.4741641337 km/h.
```

STRINGS

Strings in Python can be created using single quotes, double quotes, and triple quotes. When we use triple quotes, strings can span several lines without using the escape character.

```
#!/usr/bin/python
```

```
# strings.py

a = "keep silent"

b = 'voice'

c = """

requiem

for

a

tower

"""

print a

print b

print c
```

In our example, we assign three string literals to a, b, and c variables. And we print them to the console.

Output:

```
$ ./strings.py
keep silent
voice
```

String multiplication and concatenation:

```
#!/usr/bin/python
# strings2.py
print "good " * 5
print "good " "night"
print "good " + "and " + "night"
```

The * operator repeats the string n times. In our case five times. Two string literals next to each other are automatically concatenated. We can also use the + operator to explicitly concatenate the strings.

Output:

```
$ ./strings2.py
good good good good good
good night
good and night
```

TUPLES

A tuple is an immutable sequence data type. The tuple can contain mixed data types.

Example:

```
fruits = ("oranges", "oranges", "apples")
```

Tuples are created using round brackets. Here we have a tuple consisting of three fruit types.

```
fruits = "oranges", "oranges", "apples"

print fruits  # prints  ('oranges', 'oranges', 'apples')
```

The parentheses are not mandatory. We can omit them.

```
#!/usr/bin/python

# tuples.py

first = (1, 2, 3)

second = (4, 5, 6)

print "len(first) : ", len(first)

print "max(first) : ", max(first)

print "min(first) : ", min(first)

print "first + second :", first + second
```

```
print "first * 3 : ", first * 3

print "1 in first : ", 1 in first

print "5 not in second : ", 5 not in second
```

This example shows several basic operations with tuples. The len() function returns the number of elements in the first tuple. The max() function returns the maximum value, the min() minimum value. The addition operator adds two tuples, the multiplication operator multiplies the tuple. The in operator determines if the values are in the tuple.

Output:

```
$ ./tuples.py

len(first) :  3

max(first) :  3

min(first) :  1
```

```
first + second : (1, 2, 3, 4, 5, 6)

first * 3 : (1, 2, 3, 1, 2, 3, 1, 2, 3)

1 in first : True

5 not in second : False
```

LISTS

A list is a mutable sequence data type. The list can contain mixed data types. A list and a tuple share many common features. Because a list is a modifiable data type, it has some additional operations. A whole chapter is dedicated to the Python list.

The list is created using the square brackets [].

```
#!/usr/bin/python

# list.py
```

```
num = [0, 2, 5, 4, 6, 7]

print num[0]

print num[2:]

print len(num)

print num + [8, 9]
```

As we have stated previously, we can use the same operations on lists as on tuples.

Output

```
$ ./list.py

0

[5, 4, 6, 7]

6

[0, 2, 5, 4, 6, 7, 8, 9]
```

Counting elements in a list is done with the count() method.

```
#!/usr/bin/python

# counting.py

numbers = [5, 5, 2, 8, 8, 8, 8]

print "five is here ",  numbers.count(0),
"times"

print "one is here ",   numbers.count(1),
"times"

print "two is here ",   numbers.count(2),
"time"

print "eight is here ", numbers.count(3),
"times"
```

The script counts number occurrences in a list.

Output

```
$ ./counting.py

five is here  2 times

one is here  0 times

two is here  1 time

eight is here  4 times
```

Inserting and deleting items from the list.

```
#!/usr/bin/python

# modify.py

names = []

names.append("Melissa")

names.append("Shavonne")
```

```
names.append("Joseph")
names.append("Rebecca")
print names
names.insert(0, "Adriana")
print names
names.remove("Melissa")
names.remove("Shavonne")
del names[1]
print names
del names[0]
print names
```

Output

```
$ ./modify.py
['Melissa', 'Shavonne', 'Joseph', 'Rebecca']
```

```
['Adriana', 'Melissa', 'Shavonne', 'Joseph',
'Rebecca']

['Adriana', 'Rebecca']

['Rebecca']
```

SETS

Set is an unordered collection of data with no duplicate elements. Set supports operations like union, intersection, or difference.

Example:

```
#!/usr/bin/python

# sets.py

set1 = set(['a', 'b', 'c', 'c', 'd'])

set2 = set(['a', 'b', 'x', 'y', 'z'])
```

```
print "set1: " , set1

print "set2: " , set2

print "intersection: ", set1 & set2

print "union: ", set1 | set2

print "difference: ", set1 - set2

print "symmetric difference: ", set1 ^ set2
```

Output

```
$ ./sets.py

set1: set(['a', 'c', 'b', 'd'])

set2: set(['a', 'x', 'b', 'y', 'z'])

intersection: set(['a', 'b'])

union: set(['a', 'c', 'b', 'd', 'y', 'x', 'z'])

difference: set(['c', 'd'])

symmetric difference: set(['c', 'd', 'y', 'x',
'z'])
```

DICTIONARIES

A Python dictionary is a group of key-value pairs. The elements in a dictionary are indexed by keys. Keys in a dictionary are required to be unique. Because of the importance of the dictionary data type, a whole chapter covers the dictionary in this Python tutorial.

Example:

```
#!/usr/bin/python

# dict.py

words = { 'boy': 'Friend', 'College': 'Haus',
'death': 'Tod' }

print words['College']

print words.keys()

print words.values()

print words.items()
```

```
print words.pop('boy')

print words

words.clear()

print words
```

Output

```
$ ./dict.py

Haus

['College', 'boy', 'death']

['Haus', 'Friend', 'Tod']

[('College', 'Haus'), ('boy', 'Friend'),
('death', 'Tod')]

Friend

{'College': 'Haus', 'death': 'Tod'}

{}
```

SEQUENCE

Lists, tuples and strings are examples of sequences, but what are sequences and what is so special about them? The major features are membership tests and indexing operations, which allow us to fetch a particular Product in the sequence directly. The three types of sequences mentioned above - lists, tuples and strings, also have a slicing operation which allows us to retrieve a slice of the sequence i.e. a part of the sequence.

Example (save as ds_seq.py):

```
shoplist = ['Bag', 'Purse', 'Shoes', 'Mobile']

name = 'swaroop'

# Indexing or 'Subscription' operation #

print 'Product 0 is', shoplist[0]

print 'Product 1 is', shoplist[1]
```

```
print 'Product 2 is', shoplist[2]

print 'Product 3 is', shoplist[3]

print 'Product -1 is', shoplist[-1]

print 'Product -2 is', shoplist[-2]

print 'Character 0 is', name[0]

# Slicing on a list #

print 'Product 1 to 3 is', shoplist[1:3]

print 'Product 2 to end is', shoplist[2:]

print 'Product 1 to -1 is', shoplist[1:-1]

print 'Product start to end is', shoplist[:]

# Slicing on a string #

print 'characters 1 to 3 is', name[1:3]

print 'characters 2 to end is', name[2:]

print 'characters 1 to -1 is', name[1:-1]

print 'characters start to end is', name[:]
```

Output:

```
$ python ds_seq.py

Product 0 is Bag

Product 1 is Purse

Product 2 is Shoes

Product 3 is Mobile

Product -1 is Mobile

Product -2 is Shoes

Character 0 is s

Product 1 to 3 is ['Purse', 'Shoes']

Product 2 to end is ['Shoes', 'Mobile']

Product 1 to -1 is ['Purse', 'Shoes']

Product start to end is ['Bag', 'Purse',
'Shoes', 'Mobile']

characters 1 to 3 is wa

characters 2 to end is aroop
```

```
characters 1 to -1 is waroo

characters start to end is swaroop
```

REFERENCES

When you create an object and assign it to a variable, the variable only refers to the object and does not represent the object itself! That is, the variable name points to that part of your computer's memory where the object is stored. This is called binding the name of the object.

Generally, you don't need to be worried about this, but there is a subtle effect due to references which you need to be aware of:

Example (save as ds_reference.py):

print 'Simple Assignment'

ShoppingList = ['apple', 'Shoes', 'Purse', 'Mobile']

mylist is just another name pointing to the same object!

mylist = ShoppingList

I purchased the first item, so I remove it from the list

del ShoppingList[0]

print 'ShoppingList is', ShoppingList

print 'mylist is', mylist

Notice that both ShoppingList and mylist both print

the same list without the 'apple' confirming that

they point to the same object

print 'Copy by making a full slice'

```
# Make a copy by doing a full slice
mylist = ShoppingList[:]
# Remove first item
del mylist[0]
print 'ShoppingList is', ShoppingList
print 'mylist is', mylist
# Notice that now the two lists are different
```

Output:

```
$ python ds_reference.py
Simple Assignment
ShoppingList is ['Shoes', 'Purse', 'Mobile']
mylist is ['Shoes', 'Purse', 'Mobile']
Copy by making a full slice
ShoppingList is ['Shoes', 'Purse', 'Mobile']
mylist is ['Purse', 'Mobile']
```

PYTHON OPERATORS

Operators are functionality that does something and can be represented by symbols such as + or by special keywords. Operators require some data to operate on and such data is called operands.

Example:

5 + 1

Here 2 and 3 are operands and + is operator.

For example, to test the expression 5 + 1, use the interactive Python interpreter prompt:

```
>>> 5 + 1
6
```

```
>>> 2 * 4
8
>>>
```

Python language supports the following types of operators.

- Arithmetic Operators

- Comparison (i.e., Relational) Operators

- Assignment Operators

- Logical Operators

- Bitwise Operators

- Membership Operators

- Identity Operators

Let us assume variable a = 10 and variable b = 5, then:

Overview of the arithmetic operators:

Operator	Description	Example
+	Addition - Adds values on either side of the operator	a + b will give 15
-	Subtraction - Subtracts right hand operand from left hand operand	a - b will give 5
*	Multiplication - Multiplies values on either side of the operator	a * b will give 50
/	Division - Divides left hand operand by right hand operand	b / a will give 2
%	Modulus - Divides left hand operand by right hand operand and returns remainder	b % a will give 0
**	Exponent - Performs exponential (power) calculation on operators	a**b will give 10 to the power 5
//	Floor Division - The division of operands where the result is the quotient in which the digits after the decimal point are removed.	7//2 is equal to 3 and 7.0//2.0 is equal to 3.0

Python Comparison Operators:

Operator	Description	Example
==	Checks if the value of two operands are equal or not, if yes then condition becomes true.	(a == b) is not true.
!=	Checks if the value of two operands are equal or not, if values are not equal then condition becomes true.	(a != b) is true.
<>	Checks if the value of two operands are equal or not, if values are not equal then condition becomes true.	(a <> b) is true. This is similar to != operator.
>	Checks if the value of left operand is greater than the value of right operand, if yes then condition becomes true.	(a > b) is true.
<	Checks if the value of left operand is less than the value of right operand, if yes then condition becomes true.	(a < b) is not true.
>=	Checks if the value of left operand is greater than or equal to the value of right operand, if yes then condition becomes true.	(a >= b) is true.
<=	Checks if the value of left operand is less than or equal to the value of right operand, if yes then condition becomes true.	(a <= b) is not true.

Python Assignment Operators:

Operator	Description	Example
=	Simple assignment operator, Assigns values from right side operands to left side operand	c= a + b will assigned value of a + b into c
+=	Add AND assignment operator, It adds right operand to the left operand and assign the result to left operand	c+= a is equivalent to c= c + a
-=	Subtract AND assignment operator, It subtracts right operand from the left operand and assign the result to left operand	c-= a is equivalent to c= c - a
*=	Multiply AND assignment operator, It multiplies right operand with the left operand and assign the result to left operand	c*= a is equivalent to c= c * a
/=	Divide AND assignment operator, It divides left operand with the right operand and assign the result to left operand	c/= a is equivalent to c= c / a
%=	Modulus AND assignment operator, It takes modulus using two operands and assign the result to left operand	c%= a is equivalent to c= c % a
**=	Exponent AND assignment operator, Performs exponential (power) calculation on operators	c**= a is equivalent to c= c ** a

Python Bitwise Operators:

Bitwise operator works on bits and performs bit by bit operation.

Example:

If a = 60; and b = 13; in binary format they will be written as:

a = 0011 1100

b = 0000 1101

a&b = 0000 1100

a|b = 0011 1101

a^b = 0011 0001

~a = 1100 0011

Python Bitwise Operators:

Operator	Description	Example
&	Binary AND Operator copies a bit to the result if it exists in both operands.	(a & b) will give 12 which is 0000 1100
|	Binary OR Operator copies a bit if it exists in either operand.	(a | b) will give 61 which is 0011 1101
^	Binary XOR Operator copies the bit if it is set in one operand but not both.	(a ^ b) will give 49 which is 0011 0001
~	Binary Ones Complement Operator is unary and has the effect of 'flipping' bits.	(~a) will give -61 which is 1100 0011 in 2's complement form due to a signed binary number.
<<	Binary Left Shift Operator. The left operands value is moved left by the number of bits specified by the right operand.	a << 2 will give 240 which is 1111 0000

Python Logical Operators:

Operator	Description	Example
And	Called Logical AND operator. If both the operands are true then condition becomes true.	(a and b) is true.
Or	Called Logical OR Operator. If any of the two operands are non zero then condition becomes true.	(a or b) is true.
not	Called Logical NOT Operator. Use to reverses the logical state of its operand. If a condition is true then Logical NOT operator will make false.	not(a and b) is false.

Python Membership Operators:

Python has membership operators test for membership in a sequence, such as strings, lists, or tuples. There are two membership operators explained below:

Operator	Description	Example
In	Evaluates to true if it finds a variable in the specified sequence and false otherwise.	x in y, here in results in a 1 if x is a member of sequence y.
not in	Evaluates to true if it does not finds a variable in the specified sequence and false otherwise.	x not in y, here not in results in a 1 if x is not a member of sequence y.

Python Identity Operators:

Identity operators compare the memory locations of two objects. There are two Identity operators explained below:

Operator	Description	Example
is	Evaluates to true if the variables on either side of the operator point to the same object and false otherwise.	x is y, here is results in 1 if id(x) equals id(y).
is not	Evaluates to false if the variables on either side of the operator point to the same object and true otherwise.	x is not y, here is not results in 1 if id(x) is not equal to id(y).

Python Operators Precedence

The following table lists all operators from highest precedence to lowest.

Operator	Description
**	Exponentiation (raise to the power)
~ + -	Complement, unary plus and minus (method names for the last two are +@ and -@)
* / % //	Multiply, divide, modulo and floor division
+ -	Addition and subtraction
>> <<	Right and left bitwise shift
&	Bitwise 'AND'
^ |	Bitwise exclusive `OR' and regular `OR'
<= < > >=	Comparison operators
<> == !=	Equality operators
= %= /= //= -= += *= **=	Assignment operators
is is not	Identity operators
in not in	Membership operators
not or and	Logical operators

CONTROL FLOWS IN PYTHON

In the python programs what will you do if you want the program to take some decisions and do different things depending on different situations? Decision making structures require that the programmer specify one or more conditions to be evaluated or tested by the program, along with a statement or statements to be executed if the condition is determined to be true, and optionally, other statements to be executed if the condition is determined to be false.

There are 3 control flow statements in Python –

- **If**
- **For**
- **While**

The 'If' Statement

It is used to check a condition: if the condition is true, we run a block of statements (if-block), else we process another block of statements (else-block).

Format of If statement:

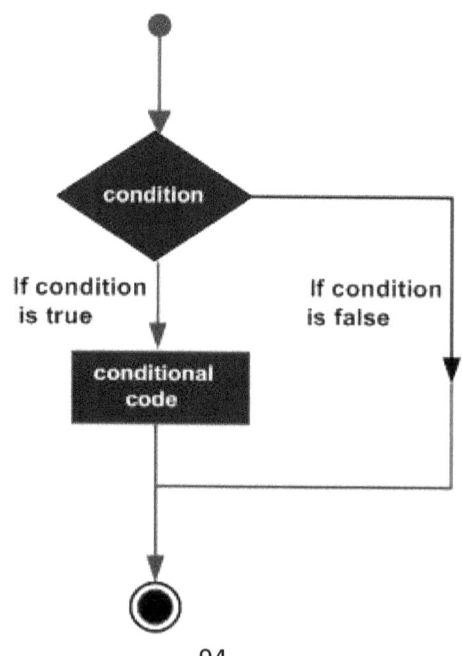

Example (save as if.py):

```
number = 40

guess = int(raw_input('Enter an integer :
'))

if guess == number:

   print 'Hello! Good Morning.'

   print '(Have a Good day!)'

elif guess < number:

   print 'Hey! Good Night'

else:

   print 'I am sleeping now.'

print 'Done'
```

Output:

```
$ python if.py

Enter an integer : 55
```

```
I am sleeping now.

Done

$ python if.py

Enter an integer : 12

Hey! Good Night

Done

$ python if.py

Enter an integer : 40

Hello! Good Morning

(Have a Good day!)

Done
```

Note that the 'if' statement contains a colon at the end. The 'elif' and else statements must also have a colon at the end of the logical line followed by their corresponding block of statements. You can have another if statement inside the if-block of an if statement and so on, this is called a nested if statement.

After Python has finished executing the complete if statement along with the associated 'elif' and 'else' clauses, it moves on to the next statement in the block containing the if statement. In this case, it is the main block, and the next statement is the print 'Done' statement. After this, Python sees the ends of the program and simply finishes up.

The 'While' Statement

Repeats a statement or group of statements while a given condition is true. It tests the condition before executing the loop body.

The structure of While Loop:

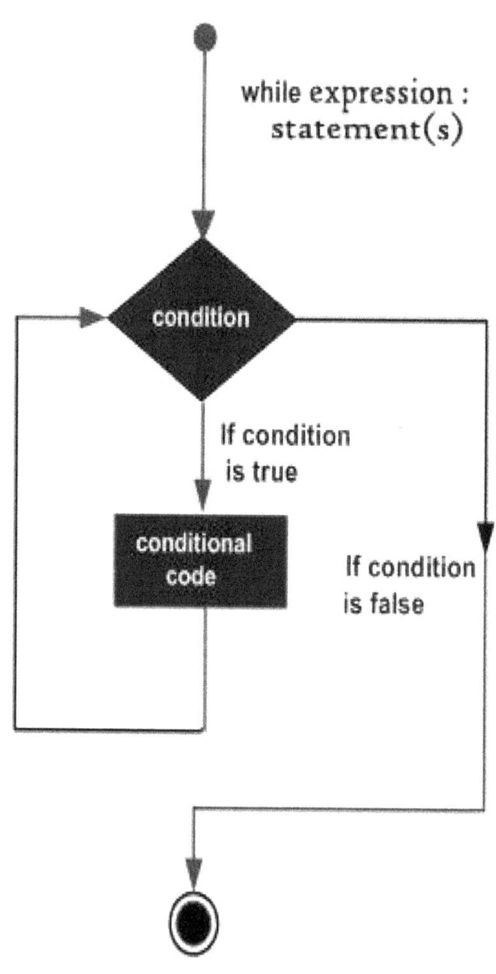

Example (save as while.py):

```
number = 40

running = True

while running:

  guess = int(raw_input('Enter an integer
: '))

  if guess == number:

    print 'Have a good day.'

    running = False

  elif guess < number:

    print 'Watching Movie..'

  else:

    print 'Good day'

else:

  print 'Take Care'

  # Do anything else you want to do here
```

```
print 'Done'
```

Output:

```
$ python while.py

Enter an integer : 55

Good day

Enter an integer : 18

Watching Movie..

Enter an integer : 40

Have a good day.

Take Care

Done
```

The else block is executed when the while loop condition becomes False, this may even be the first time that the condition is checked. If there is an else clause for a while loop, it is always executed unless you break out of the loop with a break statement. The True and False is called Boolean types and you can consider them to be equivalent to the value 1 and 0 respectively.

The 'For' Loop

The 'for' loop iterates over a sequence of objects, i.e. go through each item in a sequence. It executes a sequence of statements multiple times and abbreviates the code that manages the loop variable.

<u>The structure of For Loop:</u>

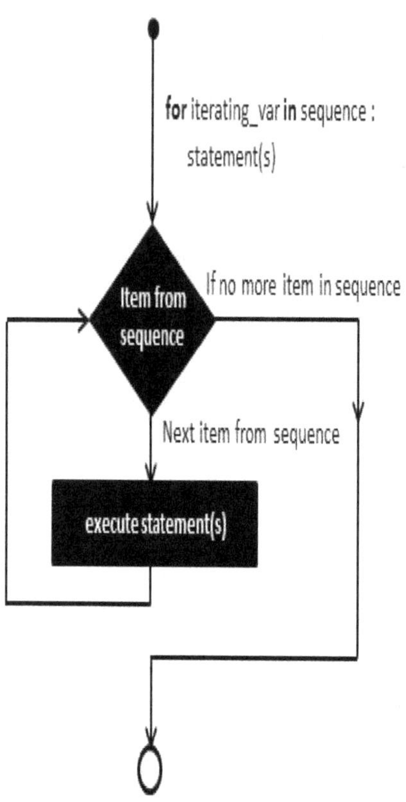

Example (save as for.py):

```
for i in range(1, 5):
    print i
else:
```

```
print 'This is the end.'
```

Output:

```
$ python for.py
1
2
3
4
This is the end.
```

Note that range() generates a sequence of numbers, but it will generate only one number at a time, when the for loop requests for the next item. If you want to see the full sequence of numbers immediately, use list(range()).

The for loop, then iterates over this range - for i in range(1,5) is equivalent to for i in [1, 2, 3, 4] which is like assigning each number (or object) in the sequence to i, one at a time, and then executing the block of statements for each value of i. In this case, we just print the value in the block of statements. Remember that the else part is optional. When included, it is always executed once after 'This is the end'. Unless a break statement is encountered. Remember that the 'for' in loop works for any sequence.

The 'Break' Statement

The break statement in Python terminates the current loop and resumes execution at the next statement, just like the traditional break found in C. The most common use for a break is when some external condition is triggered requiring a hasty exit from a loop. The break statement can be used in both while and for loops. If you are using nested loops (i.e., one loop inside another loop), the break statement will stop the execution of the innermost loop and start executing the next line of code after the block.

The break statement structure:

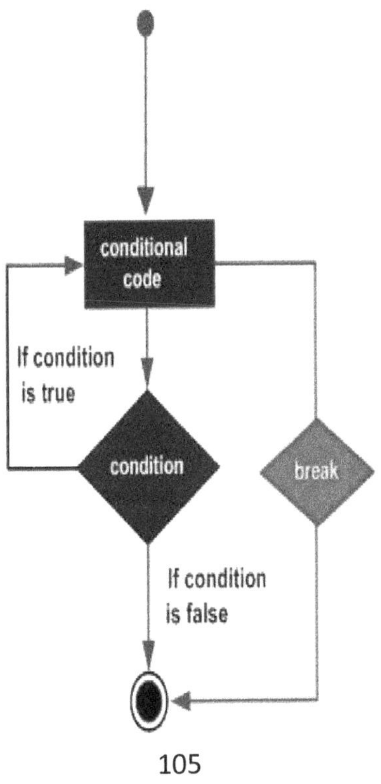

Example (save as break.py):

```
while True:
    s = raw_input('Input Text : ')
    if s == 'quit':
        break
    print 'Text length is', len(s)
print 'Done'
```

Output:

```
$ python break.py
Input Text : I am very happy
Text length is 15
Input Text : Are you ready to go
Text length is 19
Input Text : You are looking very pretty!
Text length is 28
```

```
Input Text : Python is easy:

Text length is 15

Input Text : quit

Done
```

The length of the input string can be found out using the built-in len function. Remember that the break statement can be used with the 'for loop' as well.

The Continue Statement

The continue statement in Python returns the control to the beginning of the while loop. The continue statement rejects all the remaining statements in the current iteration of the loop and moves the control back to the top of the loop. The continue statement can be used in both while and for loops.

Continue Statement Structure

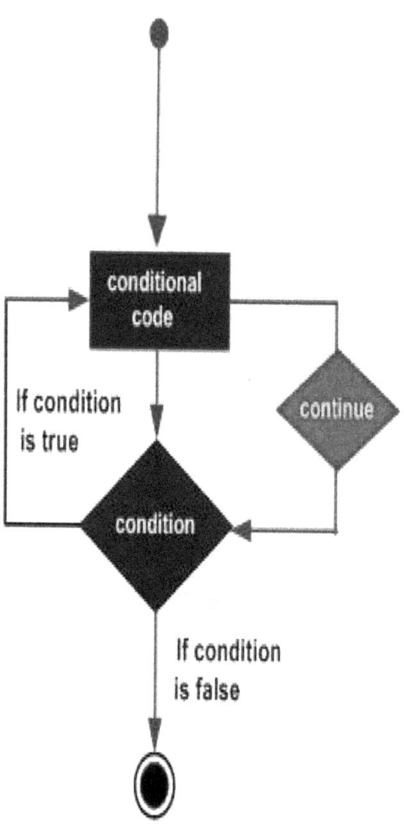

Example (save as continue.py):

```
while True:
    s = raw_input('Insert Text : ')
```

```
    if s == 'quit':
        break
    if len(s) < 5:
        print 'Too small'
        continue
    print 'Text length is sufficient'
```

Output:

```
$ python continue.py
Insert Text : sam
Too small
Insert Text : 0141
Too small
Insert Text : Alright
Text length is sufficient
Insert Text : quit
```

Note that the continue statement works with the for loop as well.

The Pass Statement

The pass statement in Python is used when a statement is required syntactically, but you don't want any command or code to execute. This is a null operation; nothing happens when it executes. The pass is also useful in places where your code will eventually go, but has not been written yet (e.g., in stubs for example):

Syntax:

The syntax for a pass statement in Python is : 'pass'

Example:

```
#!/usr/bin/python
for letter in 'Learn':
  if letter == 'a':
    pass
    print 'This is pass block'
  print 'Current Letter :', letter
print "This is so easy."
```

Output:

```
Current Letter : L
Current Letter : E
This is pass block
Current Letter : A
Current Letter : R
Current Letter : N
This is so easy.
```

PYTHON DATE & TIME

A Python program can handle dates & time in several ways. Python's time and calendar modules help track dates and times. The time intervals are floating-point numbers in units of seconds. There is a popular time module available in Python, which provides functions for working with the times, and for converting between representations. The function time.time() returns the current system time in ticks since 12:00am, January 1, 1970 (epoch).

Example:

```
#!/usr/bin/python

import time;

ticks = time.time()
```

```
print "Number of ticks since 12:00am, January 1, 1970:", ticks
```

Output:

```
Number of ticks since 12:00am, January 1, 1970: 7186862.73399
```

Getting Current Time

To translate a time instant from seconds since the epoch floating-point value into a time-tuple, pass the floating-point value to a function (e.g., localtime) that returns a time-tuple with all nine items valid.

```
#!/usr/bin/python

import time;

localtime = time.localtime(time.time())
```

```
print "Local current time :", localtime
```

Output:

```
Local current time :
time.struct_time(tm_year=2013,
tm_mon=7,

tm_mday=17, tm_hour=21, tm_min=26,
tm_sec=3, tm_wday=2, tm_yday=198,
tm_isdst=0)
```

Getting Formatted Time

You can format any time as per your requirement, but simple method to get time in readable format is asctime():

```
#!/usr/bin/python

import time;
```

```
localtime = time.asctime(
time.localtime(time.time()) )

print "Local current time :", localtime
```

Output:

```
Local current time : Tue Jan 13 10:17:09
2009
```

Getting Calendar For A Month

The calendar module gives a wide range of methods to play with yearly and monthly calendars. Here, we print a calendar for a given month (Jan 2008):

```
#!/usr/bin/python

import calendar

cal = calendar.month(2008, 1)
```

```
print "Here is the calendar:"

print cal;
```

Output:

```
Here is the calendar:

    January 2008

Mo Tu We Th Fr Sa Su

    1  2  3  4  5  6

 7  8  9 10 11 12 13

14 15 16 17 18 19 20

21 22 23 24 25 26 27

28 29 30 31
```

PYTHON FUNCTIONS

Functions in Python have equal status with other objects in Python. Functions can be assigned to variables, stored in collections or passed as arguments. This brings additional flexibility to the language.

There are two basic types of functions. Built-in functions and user defined ones. The built-in functions are part of the Python language. Examples are: dir(), len() or abs(). The user defined functions are functions created with the def keyword.

<u>The advantages of using functions are:</u>

- **Reducing duplication of code**
- **Decomposing complex problems into simpler pieces**
- **Improving clarity of the code**
- **Reuse of code**
- **Information hiding**

Functions are reusable programs, they allow you to give a name to a block of statements, allowing you to run that block using the specified name anywhere in your program and any number of times. This is known as calling the function.

Define A Function

You can define functions to provide the required functionality. Here are simple rules to define a function in Python.

- Function blocks begin with the keyword def followed by the function name and parentheses (( )).
- Any input parameters or arguments should be placed within these parentheses. You can also define parameters inside these parentheses.
- The first statement of a function can be an optional statement - the documentation string of the function or docstring.

- The code block within every function starts with a colon (:) and is indented.
- The statement return [expression] exits a function, optionally passing back an expression to the caller. A return statement with no arguments is the same as return None.

SYNTAX:

```
def functionname( parameters ):
  "function_docstring"
  function_suite
  return [expression]
```

Calling A Function

Once the basic structure of a function is finalized, you can call a function from another function or directly from the Python prompt and can execute it. Following is the example to call printme() function:

```
#!/usr/bin/python

# Function definition is here

def printme( str ):

  "This prints a passed string into this function"

  print str;

  return;

printme("I am very happy today!");

printme("This is a memorable day.");
```

Output:

```
I am very happy today!

This is a memorable day.
```

Pass By Reference In Function

All parameters in the Python language are passed by reference. It means if you change what parameter refers to within a function, then change will take place in calling function as well.

For example:

```
#!/usr/bin/python

# Function definition is here

def changeme( mylist ):
```

```
  "This changes a passed list into this function"
  mylist.append([10,20,30,40]);
  print "Enter values inside function: ", mylist
  return
# Now you can call changeme function
mylist = [1,2,3];
changeme( mylist );
print "Enter values outside function: ", mylist
```

Output:

```
Enter values inside function:  [1, 2, 3, [10,20,30,40]]
Enter values outside function:  [1, 2, 3, [10,20,30,40]]
```

The Return Statement

The statement return [expression] exits a function, optionally passing back an expression to the caller. A return statement with no arguments is the same as return None. The return statement is used to return from a function i.e. break out of the function. We can optionally return a value from the function as well.

Example (save as function_return.py):

```
def maximum(x, y):
    if x > y:
        return x
    elif x == y:
        return 'Numbers are equal'
    else:
```

```
    return y
print maximum(5, 7)
```

Output:

```
$ python function_return.py
7
```

Python Lambda Function

Other Function used in Python is Lambda Function. You can use the lambda keyword to create small anonymous functions. These functions are called anonymous because they are not declared in the standard manner by using the def keyword.

- Lambda forms can take any number of arguments, but return just one value in the form of an expression. They cannot contain commands or multiple expressions.

- An anonymous function cannot be a direct call to print because lambda requires an expression.

- Lambda functions have their own local namespace and cannot access variables other than those in their parameter list and those in the global namespace.

- Although it appears that lambda's are a one-line version of a function, they are not equivalent to inline statements in C or C++, whose purpose is by passing function stack allocation during invocation for performance reasons.

Example:

```
#!/usr/bin/python

# Function definition is here

sum = lambda arg1, arg2: arg1 + arg2;
```

```
# Now you can call sum as a function

print "Value of total : ", sum( 25, 20 )

print "Value of total : ", sum( 30, 25 )
```

Output:

```
Value of total :  45

Value of total :  55
```

PYTHON ARGUMENTS AND PARAMETERS

Python Parameters

A function can take parameters, which are values you supply to the function so that the function can do something utilizing those values. These parameters are just like variables except that the values of these variables are defined when we call the function and are already assigned values when the function runs.

Parameters are specified within the pair of parentheses in the function definition, separated by commas. When we call the function, we supply the values in the same way. Note the terminology used - the names given in the function definition are called parameters, whereas the values you supply in the function call are called arguments.

Function Parameter Example:

(save as function_param.py):

```
def print_max(a, b):
    if a > b:
        print a, 'is maximum'
    elif a == b:
        print a, 'is equal to', b
    else:
        print b, 'is maximum'
# directly pass literal values
print_max(5, 7)
x = 9
y = 13
```

```
# pass variables as arguments

print_max(x, y)
```

Output:

```
$ python function_param.py

7 is maximum

13 is maximum
```

Function Arguments:

You can call a function by using the following types of formal arguments:

- **Required arguments**
- **Keyword arguments**
- **Default arguments**
- **Variable-length arguments**

Required arguments:

Required arguments are passed to a function incorrect positional order. To call the function printme(), you definitely need to pass one argument, otherwise it would give a syntax error as follows:

SYNTAX

```
#!/usr/bin/python

# Function definition is here

def printme( str ):

  "This prints a passed string into this function"

  print str;

  return;

# Now you can call printme function

printme();
```

Output:

```
Traceback (most recent call last):
  File "test.py", line 11, in <module>
    printme();
TypeError: printme() takes exactly 1
argument (0 given)
```

Keyword arguments:

Keyword arguments relate to the function calls. When you use keyword arguments in a function call, the caller identifies the arguments by the parameter name. This allows you to skip arguments or place them out of order because the Python interpreter is able to use the keywords provided to match the values with parameters. You can also make keyword calls to the printme() function in the following ways:

Example (save as function_keyword.py):

```
def func(a, b=5, c=10):
   print 'a is', a, 'and b is', b, 'and c is', c
func(3, 7)
func(25, c=24)
func(c=50, a=100)
```

Output:

```
$ python function_keyword.py
a is 3 and b is 7 and c is 10
a is 25 and b is 5 and c is 24
a is 100 and b is 5 and c is 50
```

Default arguments:

A default argument is an argument that assumes a default value if a value is not provided in the function call in that argument. Following example gives an idea of default arguments, it would print default age if it is not passed:

Example (save as function_default.py):

```
def say(message, times=1):
   print message * times
say('Hello')
say('World', 5)
```

Output:

```
$ python function_default.py
Hello
WorldWorldWorldWorldWorld
```

Variable-length Arguments:

You may need to process a function for more arguments than you specified while defining the function. These arguments are called variable-length arguments and are not named in the function definition, unlike required and default arguments. The general syntax for a function with non-keyword variable arguments is this:

```
def functionname([formal_args,] *var_args_tuple ):
  "function_docstring"
  function_suite
  return [expression]
```

An asterisk (*) is placed before the variable name that will hold the values of all nonkeyword variable arguments. This tuple remains empty if no additional arguments are specified during the function call.

Example:

```
#!/usr/bin/python

# Function definition is here

def printinfo( arg1, *vartuple ):

  "This prints a variable passed arguments"

  print "Result is: "

  print arg1

  for var in vartuple:

    print var

  return;

# Now you can call printinfo function

printinfo( 23 );

printinfo( 15, 25, 35 );
```

Output:

```
Result is:
23
Result is:
15
25
35
```

GLOBAL AND LOCAL VARIABLES IN PYTHON

Variables that are defined inside a function body have a local scope, and those definitions outside have a global scope. This means that local variables can be accessed only inside the function in which they are declared, whereas global variables can be accessed throughout the program body by all functions. When you call a function, the variables declared inside it are brought into scope.

LOCAL VARIABLES

When you declare variables inside a function definition, they are not related in any way to other variables with the same names used outside the function - i.e. variable names are local to the function. This is called the scope of the variable. All variables have the scope of the block they are declared in starting from the point of definition of the name.

Example (save as function_local.py):

```
x = 50

def func(x):

   print 'x is', x

   x = 2

   print 'Changed local x to', x

func(x)

print 'x is still', x
```

Output:

```
$ python function_local.py

x is 50

Changed local x to 2

x is still 50
```

GLOBAL VARIABLES

If you want to assign a value to a name defined at the top level of the program (i.e. not inside any kind of scope, such as functions or classes), then you have to tell Python that the name is not local, but it is global. We do this using the global statement. It is impossible to assign a value to a variable defined outside a function without the global statement.

You can use the values of such variables defined outside the function (assuming there is no variable with the same name within the function). However, this is not encouraged and should be avoided since it becomes unclear to the reader of the program as to where that variable's definition is. Using the global statement makes it amply clear that the variable is defined in an outermost block.

Example (save as function_global.py):

```
x = 50
def func():
   global x
   print 'x is', x
   x = 2
   print 'Changed global x to', x
func()
print 'Value of x is', x
```

Output:

```
$ python function_global.py
x is 50
Changed global x to 2
Value of x is 2
```

PYTHON MODULES

A module allows you to logically organize your Python code. Grouping related code into a module makes the code easier to understand and use. A module is a Python object with arbitrarily named attributes that you can bind and reference. Simply, a module is a file consisting of Python code. A module can define functions, classes and variables. A module can also include runnable code.

There are various methods of writing modules, but the simplest way is to create a file with a .py extension, that contains functions and variables. A module can be imported by another program to make use of its functionality. This is how we can use the Python standard library as well. First, we will see how to use the standard library modules.

There are several ways to manage Python code:

- **functions**
- **classes**
- **modules**
- **packages**

Example (save as module_using_sys.py):

```
import sys

print('The command line arguments are:')

for i in sys.argv:

   print i

print '\n\nThe PYTHONPATH is',
sys.path, '\n'
```

Output:

```
$ python module_using_sys.py we are arguments

The command line arguments are:

module_using_sys.py

we

are

arguments

The PYTHONPATH is ['/tmp/py',

# many entries here, not shown here

'/Library/Python/2.7/site-packages',

'/usr/local/lib/python2.7/site-packages']
```

Importing a module is a bit costly, so Python does some tricks to make it faster. One way is to make byte-compiled files with the extension .pyc, which is an intermediate form that Python transforms the program. This .pyc file is useful when you import the module the next time from a different program, it will be much faster since a portion of the processing required in importing a module is already done. Also, these files are platform-independent.

The Import Statement

You can use any Python source file as a module by executing an import statement in some other Python source file. The import has the following syntax:

```
import module1[, module2[,... moduleN]
```

When the interpreter encounters an import statement, it imports the module if the module is present in the search path. A search path is a list of directories that the interpreter searches before importing a module. For example, to import the module hello.py, you need to put the following command at the top of the script:

```
#!/usr/bin/python

# Import module support

import support

# Now you can call defined function that module as follows

support.print_func("Zara")
```

Output:

```
Hello : Zara
```

A module is loaded only once, regardless of the number of times it is imported. This prevents the module execution from happening over and over again if multiple imports occur.

The From...Import Statement

Python's from statement lets you import specific attributes from a module into the current namespace. The from...import has the following syntax:

```
from modname import name1[, name2[, ...
nameN]]
```

Example:

```
from math import sqrt

print "Square root of 16 is", sqrt(16)
```

The From...Import * Statement

It is also possible to import all names from a module into the current namespace by using the following import statement:

```
from modname import *
```

This provides an easy way to import all the items from a module into the current namespace; however, this statement should be used sparingly.

Module Names

A module name is the file name with the .py extension. When we have a file called empty.py, empty is the module name. The __name__ is a variable that holds the name of the module being referenced. The current module, the module being executed (called also the main module) has a special name: '__main__'. With this name it can be referenced from the Python code.

Example (save as module_using_name.py):

```
if __name__ == '__main__':
    print 'Run the program successfully.'
else:
    print 'Import another module'
```

Output:

```
$ python module_using_name.py
Run the program successfully.
$ python
```

```
>>> import module_using_name
Import another module
>>>
```

Locating Modules

When a module is imported the interpreter first searches for a built-in module with that name. If not found, it then searches in a list of directories given by the variable sys.path. The sys.path is a list of strings that specifies the search path for modules. It consists of the current working directory, directory names specified in the PYTHONPATH environment variable plus some additional installation dependent directories. If the module is not found, an ImportError is raised.

```
#!/usr/bin/python

import sys

import textwrap

sp = sorted(sys.path)

dnames = ', '.join(sp)

print textwrap.fill(dnames)
```

The script prints all directories from sys.path variable.

```
import textwrap
```

The textwrap module is used for easy formatting of paragraphs.

```
sp = sorted(sys.path)
```

We retrieve a list of directories from the sys.path variable and sort them.

```
dnames = ', '.join(sp)
```

Output:

```
$ ./syspath.py

/home/janbodnar/programming/python
/modules,

/usr/lib/pymodules/python2.7,
/usr/lib/python2.7, /usr/lib/python2.7

/dist-packages, /usr/lib/python2.7/dist-
packages/PIL,
```

Executing Modules

Modules can be imported into other modules or they can be also executed. Module authors often create a test suite to test the module. Only if the module is executed as a script, the __name__ attribute equals to __main__. We will demonstrate this on a Fibonacci module. Fibonacci numbers are a sequence of numbers, where each is the sum of its two immediate predecessors.

```
#!/usr/bin/python

"""

A module containing the fibonacci

function.

"""

def fib(n):

   a, b = 0, 1

   while b < n:

      print b,

      (a, b) = (b, a + b)

# testing

if __name__ == '__main__':

  fib(500)
```

The module can be normally imported as usual. The module can be also executed.

```
$ ./fibonacci.py

1 1 2 3 5 8 13 21 34 55 89 144 233 377
```

If we do import the Fibonacci module, the test is not executed automatically.

```
>>> import Fibonacci as fib

>>> fib.fib(500)

1 1 2 3 5 8 13 21 34 55 89 144 233 377
```

The Fibonacci module is imported and the fib() function is executed.

Making Your Own Modules

Creating your own modules is easy, you've been doing it all along! This is because every Python program is also a module. You just have to make sure it has a .py extension. The following example should make it clear.

Example (save as mymodule.py):

```
def say_hi():
    print 'Hi, I am learning Python.'
__version__ = '0.2.1'
```

Another module (save as mymodule_demo.py):

```
import mymodule
mymodule.say_hi()
print 'Version', mymodule.__version__
```

Output:

```
$ python mymodule_demo.py

Hi, I am learning Python.

Version 0.2.1
```

The dir() Function

The built-in dir() function gives a sorted list of strings containing the names defined by a module. The list contains the names of all the modules, variables and functions that are defined in a module.

Example:

```
#!/usr/bin/python

# Import built-in module math

import math
```

```
content = dir(math)

print content;
```

Output:

```
['__doc__', '__file__', '__name__', 'acos', 'asin',
'atan',

'atan2', 'ceil', 'cos', 'cosh', 'degrees', 'e',
'exp',

'fabs', 'floor', 'fmod', 'frexp', 'hypot',
'ldexp', 'log',

'log10', 'modf', 'pi', 'pow', 'radians', 'sin',
'sinh',

'sqrt', 'tan', 'tanh']
```

PACKAGES IN PYTHON

By now, you must have started observing the hierarchy of organizing your programs. Variables usually go inside functions. Functions and global variables usually go inside modules. Packages are just folders of modules with a special init.py file that indicates to Python that this folder is special because it contains Python modules. Let's say you want to create a package called 'world' with subpackages 'asia', 'africa', etc. and these subpackages in turn contain modules like 'india', 'madagascar', etc.

This is how you would structure the folders:

```
- <some folder present in the sys.path>/
    - world/
        - __init__.py
```

```
- asia/
    - __init__.py
    - india/
        - __init__.py
        - foo.py
- africa/
    - __init__.py
    - madagascar/
        - __init__.py
        - bar.py
```

Packages are just a convenience to hierarchically organize modules. You will see many instances of this in the standard library. A package is a hierarchical file directory structure that defines a single Python application environment that consists of modules and subpackages and sub-subpackages, and so on.

Consider a file Pots.py available in Phone directory. This file has following line of source code:

```
#!/usr/bin/python

def Pots():

  print "I'm Pots Phone"
```

Similar way, we have another two files having different functions with the same name as above:

Phone/Isdn.py file having function Isdn()

Phone/G3.py file having function G3()

Now, create one more file __init__.py in Phone directory:

Phone/__init__.py

If you want all of your functions available, you need to put explicit import statements in __init__.py as follows:

```
from Pots import Pots

from Isdn import Isdn

from G3 import G3
```

By doing so you have all of these classes available when you've imported the Phone package.

```
#!/usr/bin/python

# Now import your Phone Package.

import Phone

Phone.Pots()

Phone.Isdn()

Phone.G3()
```

Output:

```
I'm Pots Phone

I'm 3G Phone

I'm ISDN Phone
```

Python Exceptions Handling

Errors detected during execution are called exceptions. During the execution of our application, many things might go wrong. A disk might get full and we cannot save our file. An Internet connection might go down and our application tries to connect to a site. All these might result in a crash of our application. To prevent this, we must cope with all possible errors that might occur. For this, we can use the exception handling.

Python provides two very important features to handle any unexpected error in your Python programs and to add debugging capabilities to them:

- **Exception Handling**: This would be covered in this tutorial. Here is a list standard Exceptions available in Python: Standard Exceptions.

- **Assertions**: This would be covered in Assertions in Python tutorial.

SYNTAX:

```
try:
   You do your operations here;
   ......................
except ExceptionI:
   If there is ExceptionI, then execute this block.
except ExceptionII:
   If there is ExceptionII, then execute this block.
```

```
......................
else:
  If there is no exception then execute this
block.
```

Example:

Here is simple example, which opens a file and writes the content in the file and comes out gracefully because there is no problem at all:

```
#!/usr/bin/python
try:
  fh = open("testfile", "w")
  fh.write("This is my test file for
exception handling!!")
except IOError:
  print "Error: can\'t find file or read
data"
```

```
else:
   print "This is ultimate guide to learn Python."
   fh.close()
```

Output:

```
This is ultimate guide to learn Python.
```

Hierarchy Of Exceptions

The exceptions are organized in a hierarchy, being Exception the parent of all exceptions.

```
#!/usr/bin/python
# interrupt.py
try:
   while True:
```

```
    pass
except KeyboardInterrupt:
  print "Program interrupted"
```

The script starts and endless cycle. If we press Ctrl+C, we interrupt the cycle. Here, we caught the KeyboardInterrupt exception.

```
Exception
  BaseException
    KeyboardInterrupt
```

This is the hierarchy of the KeyboardInterrupt exception.

User Defined Exceptions

We can create our own exceptions if we want. We do it by defining a new exception class.

```
#!/usr/bin/python

# b.py

class BFoundError(Exception):

  def __init__(self, value):

    print "BFoundError: b character found at position %d" % value

string = "You make me want to be a better man."

pos = 0

for i in string:

  if i == 'b':

    raise BFoundError, pos

  pos = pos + 1
```

In our code example, we have created a new exception. The exception is derived from the base Exception class. If we find any occurrence of letter b in a string, we raise our exception.

Output:

```
$ ./b.py

BFoundError: b character found at
position 20

Traceback (most recent call last):

  File "./b.py", line 16, in <module>

    raise BFoundError, pos

__main__.BFoundError
```

The Cleanup

There is a finally keyword, which is always executed. No matter if the exception is raised or not. It is often used to do some cleanup of resources in a program.

```
#!/usr/bin/python

# cleanup.py

f = None

try:

  f = file('indaclub', 'r')

  contents = f.readlines()

  for i in contents:

    print i,

except IOError:

  print 'Error opening file'

finally:

  if f:

    f.close()
```

In our example, we try to open a file. If we cannot open the file, an IOError is raised. In case we opened the file, we want to close the file handler. For this, we use the finally keyword. In the finally block we check if the file is opened or not. If it is opened, we close it. This is a common programming construct when we work with databases. There we similarly cleanup the opened database connections.

SOME OTHER FUNCTIONS TO PERFORM IN PYTHON

Reading Keyboard Input

Python provides two built-in functions to read a line of text from standard input, which by default comes from the keyboard. These functions are:

- raw_input

- input

The raw_input Function:

The raw_input([prompt]) function reads one line from standard input and returns it as a string (removing the trailing newline).

```
#!/usr/bin/python

str = raw_input("Enter your input: ");

print "Received input is : ", str
```

Output:

```
Enter your input: Hello Petter

Received input is :  Hello Petter
```

The input Function:

The input([prompt]) function is equivalent to raw_input, except that it assumes the input is a valid Python expression and returns the evaluated result to you.

```
#!/usr/bin/python

str = input("Enter your input: ");
```

```
print "Received input is : ", str
```

Output:

```
Enter your input: [x*5 for x in
range(2,10,2)]

Recieved input is :  [10, 20, 30, 40]
```

Opening And Closing Files

Python provides basic functions and methods necessary to manipulate files by default. You can do your most of the file manipulation using a file object.

The open Function:

Before you can read or write a file, you have to open it using Python's built-in open() function. This function creates a file object, which would be utilized to call other support methods associated with it.

Syntax:

```
file object = open(file_name [, access_mode][, buffering])
```

Here is paramters' detail:

-> **file_name:** The file_name argument is a string value that contains the name of the file that you want to access.

-> **access_mode:** The access_mode determines the mode in which the file has to be opened, i.e., read, write, append, etc. A complete list of possible values is given below in the table. This is optional parameter and the default file access mode is read (r).

-> **buffering:** If the buffering value is set to 0, no buffering will take place. If the buffering value is 1, line buffering will be performed while accessing a file. If you specify the buffering value as an integer greater than 1, then buffering action will be performed with the indicated buffer size. If negative, the buffer size is the system default(default behavior).

List of different modes of opening a file:

Modes	Description
R	Opens a file for reading only. The file pointer is placed at the beginning of the file. This is the default mode.
Rb	Opens a file for reading only in binary format. The file pointer is placed at the beginning of the file. This is the default mode.
r+	Opens a file for both reading and writing. The file pointer will be at the beginning of the file.
rb+	Opens a file for both reading and writing in binary format. The file pointer will be at the beginning of the file.
W	Opens a file for writing only. Overwrites the file if the file exists. If the file does not exist, creates a new file for writing.
Wb	Opens a file for writing only in binary format. Overwrites the file if the file exists. If the file does not exist, creates a new file for writing.
w+	Opens a file for both writing and reading. Overwrites the existing file if the file exists. If the file does not exist, creates a new file for reading and writing.
wb+	Opens a file for both writing and reading in binary format. Overwrites the existing file if the file exists. If the file does not exist, creates a new file for reading and writing.
A	Opens a file for appending. The file pointer is at the end of the file if the file exists. That is, the file is in the append mode. If the file does not exist, it creates a new file for writing.
Ab	Opens a file for appending in binary format. The file pointer is at the end of the file if the file exists. That is, the file is in the append mode. If the file does not exist, it creates a new file for writing.
a+	Opens a file for both appending and reading. The file pointer is at the end of the file if the file exists. The file opens in the append mode. If the file does not exist, it creates a new file for reading and writing.
ab+	Opens a file for both appending and reading in binary format. The file pointer is at the end of the file if the file exists. The file opens in the append mode. If the file does not exist, it creates a new file for reading and writing.

The File Object Attributes

Here is a list of all attributes related to file object:

Attribute	Description
file.closed	Returns true if file is closed, false otherwise.
file.mode	Returns access mode with which file was opened.
file.name	Returns name of the file.
file.softspace	Returns false if space explicitly required with print, true otherwise.

Example:

```
#!/usr/bin/python

# Open a file

fo = open("foo.txt", "wb")

print "Name of the file: ", fo.name

print "Closed or not : ", fo.closed

print "Opening mode : ", fo.mode

print "Softspace flag : ", fo.softspace
```

Output:

```
Name of the file:  foo.txt

Closed or not :  False

Opening mode :  wb

Softspace flag :  0
```

The Close() Method

The close() method of a file object flushes any unwritten information and closes the file object, after which no more writing can be done.

Python automatically closes a file when the reference object of a file is reassigned to another file. It is a good practice to use the close() method to close a file.

Syntax:

```
fileObject.close();
```

Example:

```
#!/usr/bin/python

# Open a file

fo = open("foo.txt", "wb")

print "Name of the file: ", fo.name

# Close opend file

fo.close()
```

Output:

```
Name of the file:  foo.txt
```

Reading And Writing Files

The file object provides a set of access methods to make our lives easier. We would see how to use read() and write() methods to read and write files.

The write() Method:

The write() method writes any string to an open file. It is important to note that Python strings can have binary data and not just text. The write() method does not add a newline character ('\n') to the end of the string:

Syntax:

```
fileObject.write(string);
```

Example:

```
#!/usr/bin/python
```

```
# Open a file

fo = open("foo.txt", "wb")

fo.write( "Python is a great
language.\nYeah its great!!\n");

# Close opend file

fo.close()
```

Output:

```
Python is a great language.

Yeah its great!!
```

The Read() Method

The read() method reads a string from an open file. It is important to note that Python strings can have binary data and not just text.

Syntax:

```
fileObject.read([count]);
```

Example:

```
#!/usr/bin/python
# Open a file
fo = open("foo.txt", "r+")
str = fo.read(10);
print "Read String is : ", str
# Close opend file
fo.close()
```

Output:

```
Read String is :  Python is
```

Renaming And Deleting Files

Python OS module provides methods that help you perform file-processing operations, such as renaming and deleting files. To use this module you need to import it first and then you can call any related functions.

The Rename() Method

The rename() method takes two arguments, the current filename and the new filename.

Syntax:

```
os.rename(current_file_name,
new_file_name)
```

Example:

```
#!/usr/bin/python
```

```
import os

# Rename a file from test1.txt to test2.txt

os.rename( "test1.txt", "test2.txt" )
```

The Remove() Method

You can use the remove() method to delete files by supplying the name of the file to be deleted as the argument.

Syntax:

```
os.remove(file_name)
```

Example:

```
#!/usr/bin/python

import os

# Delete file test2.txt

os.remove("text2.txt")
```

Directories In Python

All files are contained within various directories, and Python has no problem handling these too. The os module has several methods that help you create, remove and change directories.

The mkdir() Method:

You can use the mkdir() method of the os module to create directories in the current directory. You need to supply an argument to this method which contains the name of the directory to be created.

Syntax:

```
os.mkdir("newdir")
```

Example:

```
#!/usr/bin/python
```

```
import os
# Create a directory "test"
os.mkdir("test")
```

The chdir() Method:

You can use the chdir() method to change the current directory. The chdir() method takes an argument, which is the name of the directory that you want to make the current directory.

Syntax:

```
os.chdir("newdir")
```

Example:

```
#!/usr/bin/python
```

```
import os

# Changing a directory to
"/home/newdir"

os.chdir("/home/newdir")
```

The getcwd() Method

The getcwd() method displays the current working directory.

Syntax:

```
os.getcwd()
```

Example:

```
#!/usr/bin/python

import os
```

```
# This would give location of the current directory
os.getcwd()
```

The rmdir() Method

The rmdir() method deletes the directory, which is passed as an argument in the method.

Syntax:

```
os.rmdir('dirname')
```

Example:

```
#!/usr/bin/python
import os
```

```
# This would remove "/tmp/test" directory.
os.rmdir( "/tmp/test" )
```

This is all about basics of Python Programming Language. All data structures, functions, loops, strings, classes are define in this book with examples and their syntax. Now you can enjoy with the reading the next series of this book – "Complete Guide For Python Programming".

NOTE

This is all about basics of Python Programming. These things are must to understand if you are a beginner in learning Python Program Language. I Hope you liked the book and learned a lot from it. In my second upcoming book, I will give you introduction to How to write programs in Python and other functions of python. We will study about python programming in details Advanced structures, loops, python implementation, classes, objects, and a lot more.

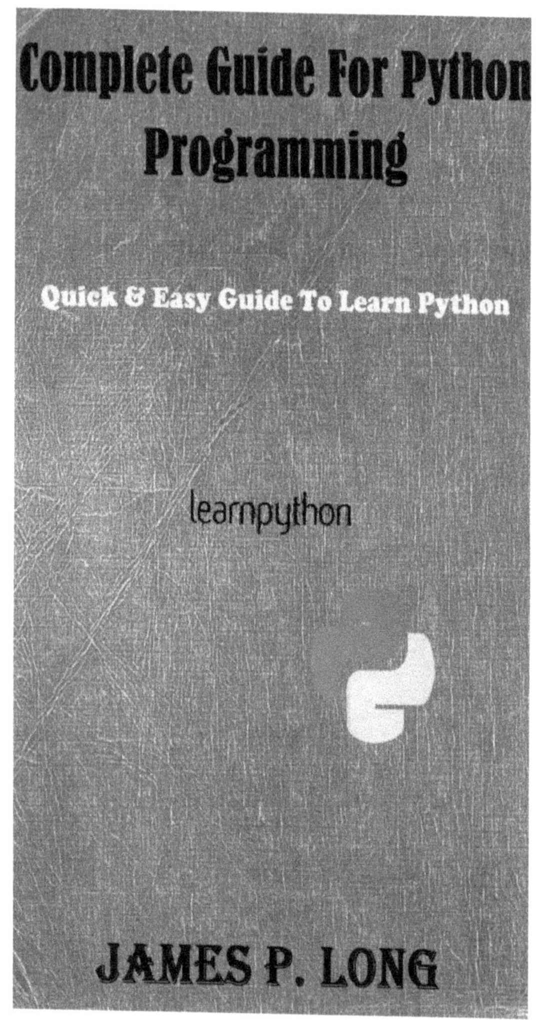
Complete Guide For Python Programming
Quick & Easy Guide To Learn Python
learnpython
JAMES P. LONG

Complete Guide For Python Programming

Quick & Easy Guide To Learn Python

By:

James P. Long

ACKNOWLEDGMENT

For my students and friends, who all selflessly helped me in writing this book. Special thanks to those who asked, insisted and assisted me in turning my ideas into this book form.

Table of Contents

INTRODUCTION

Python is a wide used general, high-level programming language. Its style philosophy emphasizes code readability, and its syntax allows programmers to precise ideas in fewer lines of code that might be possible in languages like C++ or Java. The language provides constructs supposed to modify clear programs on both small and large scales.

Python is a simple to learn, powerful programming language. Its economical high-level information structures and an easy, but effective approach to object-oriented programming. Python's elegant syntax and dynamic typing, in conjunction with its interpreted nature, make it a perfect language for scripting and speedy application development in several areas on most platforms. Python is one in all those rare languages which might claim to both easy and powerful. You may end up pleasantly stunned to examine how easy it's to think about the answer to the matter instead of the syntax and structure of the language you are programming in.

In my first book "**Python Programming for Beginners**", I have discussed all about what python programming language is? How to install python to your system? Different data types, function, parameters, class, objects used in python. I also have discussed about basic python operators and modules. Not only these, you can also get knowledge on how to call a function, exception handling function, python variables etc. That is all basic things that are must know when you start learning any programming language.

Now in this book I am going to share with you advanced python programming functions and programs to create in python? I assure you that if you go through this book seriously, then in few days you will become an expert python programmer. So what are you waiting for? Start going through the book and start creating your first program today.

PYTHON VERSIONS

Python has many versions but most commonly used are Python 2.0 and Python 3.0. Python 2.0 was released on 16 October 2000, with many major new features including a full garbage collector and support for Unicode. With this release the development process was changed and became more transparent and community-backed. while Python 3.0 , which is also known as Python 3000 or py3k, is a major, backwards-incompatible release, and was released on 3 December 2008. Many of its major features have been back ported to the backwards-compatible Python 2.6 and 2.7. Python 2.x is legacy, Python 3.x is the present and future of the language.

Python 3.0 was released in 2008. The final 2.x version 2.7 release came out in mid-2010, with a statement of extended support for this end-of-life release. The 2.x branch will see no new major releases after that. 3.x is under active development and has already seen over five years of stable releases, including version 3.3 in 2012 and 3.4 in 2014. This means that all recent standard library improvements, for example, are only available by default in Python 3.x.

For those interested in using Python via a USB thumb drive, you may be interested in Portable Python. This is a self-contained Python environment that you can either run from the thumb drive or install to your computer. This is useful for people who can't or don't want to install Python but would still like to use it.

SOME COMMONLY USED OPERATIONS IN PYTHON

Using Blank Lines:

A line containing only whitespace, possibly with a comment, is called a blank line and Python ignores it completely. In an interactive interpreter session, you must enter an empty physical line to terminate a multiline statement.

Waiting for the User:

The following line of the program displays the prompt, Press the enter key to exit and waits for the user to press the Enter key:

```
#!/usr/bin/python raw_input("\n\nPress the enter key to exit.")
```

Here, "\n\n" are being used to create two new lines before displaying the actual line. Once the user presses the key, the program ends. This is a nice trick to keep a console window open until the user is done with an application.

Multiple Statements on a Single Line:

The semicolon (;) allows multiple statements on the single line given that neither statement starts a new code block. Here is a sample snip using the semicolon:

```
import sys; a = 'abc'; sys.stdout.write(a +
'\n')
```

Multiple Statement Groups as Suites:

In Python, a group of statements, which make a single code block are called suites. Compound or complex statements, such as if, while, def, and class, are those which require a header line and a suite. Header lines begin the statement and terminates with a colon (:) and are followed by one or more lines, which make up the suite. For example:

if expression : suite

elif expression : suite

else : suite

Accessing Command--Line Arguments:

Python provides a getopt module that helps you parse command-line options and arguments.

$ python test.py arg1 arg2 arg3

The Python sys module provides access to any command-line arguments via the sys.argv. This serves two purpose:

• sys.argv is the list of command-line arguments.

• len(sys.argv) is the number of command-line arguments.

Parsing Command---Line Arguments:

Python provides a getopt module that helps you parse command-line options and arguments. This module provides two functions and an exception to enable command-line argument parsing.

getopt.getopt method:

This method parses command-line options and parameter list. Following is simple syntax for this method:

getopt.getopt(args, options[, long_options])

Here is the detail of the parameters:

• args: This is the argument list to be parsed.

• options: This is the string of option letters that the script wants to recognize, with options that require an argument should be followed by a colon (:).

• long_options: This is optional parameter and if specified, must be a list of strings with the names of the long options, which should be supported. Long options, which require an argument should be followed by an equal sign ('='). To accept only long options, options should be an empty string.

PRINTF FORMAT STRINGS

%d : integer

%5d : integer in a field of width 5 chars

%-5d : integer in a field of width 5 chars, but adjusted to the left

%05d : integer in a field of width 5 chars, padded with zeroes from the left

%g : float variable in %f or %g notation

%e : float variable in scientific notation

%11.3e : float variable in scientific notation, with 3 decimals, field of width 11 chars

%5.1f : float variable in fixed decimal notation, with one decimal, field of width 5 chars

%.3f : float variable in fixed decimal form, with three decimals, field of min. width

%s : string

%-20s : string in a field of width 20 chars, and adjusted to the left

PYTHON INTERACTIVE - USING PYTHON AS A CALCULATOR

You can use python as a calculator, as you can add, subtract, multiply and divide numbers in python language.

Start Python (or IDLE, the Python IDE).

A prompt is showing up:

```
>>>
```

Display version:

```
>>>help()
```

Welcome to Python 2.7! This is the online help utility.

```
...

help>
```

Help commands:

modules: available modules

keywords: list of reserved Python keywords

quit: leave help

To get help on a keyword, just enter its name in help.

Common Operators in Python

Operator		Example	Explication
+, - *, /	add, substract, multiply, divide		
%	modulo	25 % 5 = 0 84 % 5 = 4	25/5 = 5, remainder = 0 84/5 = 16, remainder = 4
**	exponent	2**10 = 1024	
//	floor division	84//5 = 16	84/5 = 16, remainder = 4

Example For Simple Calculations in Python

```
>>> 3.14*5
15.700000000000001
```

Take care in Python 2.x if you divide two numbers:

Isn't this strange:

```
>>> 35/6
5
```

Obviously the result is wrong!

But:

```
>>> 35.0/6
5.833333333333333
>>> 35/6.0
5.833333333333333
```

In the first example, 35 and 6 are interpreted as integer numbers, so integer division is used and the result is an integer.

This uncanny behavior has been abolished in Python 3, where 35/6 gives 5.833333333333333.

In Python 2.x, use floating point numbers (like 3.14, 3.0 etc....) to force floating point division!

PYTHON IMPLEMENTATIONS

An "implementation" of Python provides support for the execution of programs which are written in the Python Programming language, is represented by the CPython reference implementation. There several implementation to run python programs. Let's have a look at them:

CPython Variants

These are implementations which are based on the CPython runtime core, but with extended behavior or features in some aspects.

CrossTwine Linker - A combination of CPython and an add-on library offering improved performance.

Stackless Python - CPython with an emphasis on concurrency using tasklets and channels.

Unladen-Swallow - an optimization branch of CPython, intended to be fully compatible and significantly faster.

WPython - a re-implementation of CPython using "wordcode" instead of bytecode.

Other Implementations

These are re-implementations of the Python language that do not depend on the CPython runtime core. Many of them reuse the standard library implementation. The only implementations that are known to be compatible with a given version of the language are IronPython, Jython and PyPy.

The following implementations are comprehensive or even complete, that you can run typical programs with them already:

Brython - A way to run Python in the browser through translation to JavaScript.

CLPython - Python in Common Lisp.

HotPy - A virtual machine for Python supporting bytecode optimization and translation using type information gathered at run-time.

IronPython - Python in C# for the Common Language Runtime (CLR/.NET) and the FePy project's IronPython Community Edition (IPCE).

Jython - Python in Java for the Java platform.

Pyjs - A Python to JavaScript compiler plus Web/GUI framework.

PyMite - Python for embedded devices.

PyPy - Python in Python, targeting several environments.

Pyvm - A Python-related virtual machine and software suite providing a nearly self-contained "userspace" system.

RapydScript - A Python-like language that compiles to JavaScript.

SNAPpy - A subset of the Python language that has been optimized for use in low-power embedded devices.

Tinypy - A minimalist implementation of Python in 64K of code .

Tentative Implementations

The following implementations are apparent works in progress; they may not be able to run typical programs:

Berp - an implementation of Python 3 in Haskell, providing an interactive environment as well as a compiler.

Phpython - a Python interpreter written in PHP.

Pyjaco - a Python to JavaScript compiler similar to Pyjs but lighter weight.

Pystacho - is, like Skulpt, Python in JavaScript.

Pyvm2.py - a CPython bytecode interpreter written in Python.

Skulpt - Python in JavaScript.

Typhon - a Rubinius-based implementation of Python.

Python Compilers & Numerical Accelerators

Compilers

These compilers usually implement something close to Python, have a look at them:

2c-python - a static Python-to-C compiler, apparently translating CPython bytecode to C.

Compyler - an attempt to "transliterate the bytecode into x 86 assemblies".

Cython - a widely used optimizing Python-to-C compiler, CPython extension module generator, and wrapper language for binding external libraries. Interacts with CPython runtime and supports embedding CPython in stand-alone binaries.

GCC Python Front-End - an in-progress effort to compile Python code within the GCC infrastructure.

Nuitka - a Python-to-C++ compiler using libpython at run-time, attempting some compile-time and run-time optimizations. Interacts with CPython runtime.

Pyc - performs static analysis in order to compile Python programs, uses similar techniques to Shed Skin.

Shed Skin - a Python-to-C++ compiler, restricted to an implicitly statically typed subset of the language for which it can automatically infer efficient types through whole program analysis.

UnPython - a Python to C compiler using type annotations.

Numerical Accelerators

Copperhead - purely functional data-parallel Python compiles to multi-core and GPU backends.

Numba - NumPy-aware optimizing runtime compiler for Python.

Parakeet - runtime compiler for a numerical subset of Python.

Logical And Physical Line in Python

A physical line is what you see when you write the program in python. A logical line is what Python sees as a single statement. Python implicitly assumes that each physical line corresponds to a logical line. For example, you want to write - 'hello world' - if this was on a line by itself, then this also corresponds to a physical line.

If you want to specify more than one logical line on a single physical line, then you have to explicitly specify this using a semicolon (;) which indicates the end of a logical line/statement.

For example:

```
i = 12
```

```
print i
```

is effectively same as

```
i = 12;
print i;
```

which is also same as

```
i = 12; print i;
```

and same as

```
i = 12; print i
```

If you have a long line of code, you can break it into multiple physical lines by using the backslash. This is referred to as explicit line joining:

```
s = 'This is a python book. \
This continues the book.'
print s
```

Output:

```
This is a python book. This continues the
book.
```

Similarly,

```
print \
i
```

is the same as

```
print i
```

Sometimes, there is an implicit assumption where you don’t need to use a backslash. This is the case where the logical line has starting parentheses, starting square brackets or a starting curly braces but not an ending one. This is called implicit line joining. You can see this in action when we write programs using lists in later chapters.

PYTHON INDENTATION

Whitespace is very important in Python. The whitespace at the beginning of the line is called indentation. Leading whitespace at the beginning of the logical line is used to determine the indentation level of the logical line, which in turn is used to determine the grouping of statements. Each set of statements is called a block.

For example:

```
i = 5

# Error below! Notice a single space at the start of the line

 print 'Value is ', i

print 'I repeat, the value is ', i
```

When you run this, you get error:

```
File "whitespace.py", line 5
  print 'Value is ', i
  ^
IndentationError: unexpected indent
```

Notice that there is a single space at the beginning of the second line. The error indicated by Python tells us that the syntax of the program is invalid i.e. the program was not properly written. Use four spaces for indentation. This is the official Python language recommendation. Good editors will automatically do this for you. Make sure you use a consistent number of spaces for indentation; otherwise your program will show errors. Python always use indentation for blocks and will never use braces.

PYTHON STANDARD LIBRARY

The Python Standard Library contains a huge number of useful modules and is part of every standard Python installation. we will explore some of the commonly used modules in this library. You can find complete details for all of the modules in the Python Standard Library in the 'Library Reference' section of the documentation that comes with your Python installation.

sys module

The sys module contains system-specific functionality. We have already seen that the sys.argv list contains the command-line arguments. For example, you want to check the version of the Python software being used; the sys module gives us that information.

```
$ python
>>> import sys
>>> sys.version_info
sys.version_info(major=2, minor=7,
micro=6, releaselevel='final', serial=0)
>>> sys.version_info.major == 2
True
```

logging module

What if you wanted to have some debugging messages or important messages to be stored somewhere so that you can check whether your program has been running as you would expect it? How do you "store somewhere" these messages? This can be achieved using the logging module.

Save as stdlib_logging.py:

```
import os, platform, logging

if
platform.platform().startswith('Windows'):

   logging_file =
os.path.join(os.getenv('HOMEDRIVE'),

                        os.getenv('HOMEPATH'),

                        'test.log')

else:

   logging_file =
os.path.join(os.getenv('HOME'), 'test.log')

print "Logging to", logging_file

logging.basicConfig(

   level=logging.DEBUG,

   format='%(asctime)s : %(levelname)s :
%(message)s',

   filename = logging_file,
```

```
    filemode = 'w',
)
logging.debug("Start of the program")
logging.info("Doing something")
logging.warning("Dying now")
```

Output:

```
$ python stdlib_logging.py
Logging to /Users/swa/test.log
$ cat /Users/swa/test.log
2014-03-29 09:27:36,660 : DEBUG : Start of the program
2014-03-29 09:27:36,660 : INFO : Doing something
2014-03-29 09:27:36,660 : WARNING : Dying now
```

CREATING CLASSES & OBJECTS

Python is an object-oriented language and because of this creating and using classes and objects are quite easy.

Overview of OOP Terminology

Class: A user-defined prototype for an object that defines a set of attributes that characterize any object of the class. The attributes are data members and methods, accessed via dot notation.

Class variable: A variable that is shared by all instances of a class. Class variables are defined within a class but outside any of the class's methods. Class variables aren't used as frequently as instance variables are.

Data member: A class variable or instance variable that holds data associated with a class and its objects.

Function overloading: The assignment of more than one behavior to a particular function. The operation performed varies by the types of objects involved.

Instance variable: A variable that is defined inside a method and belongs only to the current instance of a class.

Inheritance: The transfer of the characteristics of a class to other classes that are derived from it.

Instance: An individual object of a certain class. An object 'obj' that belongs to a class

Circle, for example, is an instance of the class Circle.

Instantiation: The creation of an instance of a class.

Method: A special kind of function that is defined in a class definition.

Object: A unique instance of a data structure that's defined by its class. An object comprises both data members and methods.

Operator overloading: The assignment of more than one function to a particular operator.

DOCUMENTING YOUR CODE

To document a Python object, docstring is used. A docstring is simply a triple-quoted sentence which gives a brief summary of the object. The object can be anything a function, a method, a class, etc.

Anything written in the triple quotes is the function’s docstring, which documents what the function does. A docstring, is the first thing that is defined in a function. Docstring is available at runtime as an attribute of the function. The docstring of a script should be usable as its ‘usage’ message, printed when the script is invoked with incorrect or missing arguments. The docstring is a phrase ending in a period. It describes the function’s effect as a command.

In docstring for a module classes, exceptions and functions that are exported by the module are listed. The docstring for a function or method summarize its behavior and document its arguments, return value(s), side effects and exceptions raised. The docstring for a class summarize its behavior and list the public methods and instance variables. Individual methods should be documented by their own docstring.

You can add a docstring to a function, class, or module by adding a string as the first indented statement.

For example:

```
#!/usr/bin/env python

# docstringexample.py
```

```
"""Example of using documentation
strings."""

class Knight:

"""

An example class.

Call spam to get bacon.

"""

def spam(eggs="bacon"):

"""Prints the argument given."""

print(eggs)
```

PYTHON - OBJECT ORIENTED PROGRAMMING

Learning Python Classes

In OOP (object-oriented programming), the class is the most basic component. OOP is very powerful tool and many Python libraries and APIs uses classes, and so you should know what classes are? How they work? And how to create them? One thing to remember about Python and OOP is that it's not mandatory to use objects in your code.

Now the question is how are Classes Better?

Let's take an example, suppose you want to calculate the velocity of a car in a two-dimensional plane using functions. And you now want to make a new program to calculate the velocity of an airplane in three dimensions, and then you'll have to rewrite the many of the functions to make them work for the vertical dimension, especially to map the object in a 3-D space. In that case classes are used. Classes let you define an object once, and then you can reuse it multiple times. You need to give it a base function, and then build upon that method to redefine it as necessary.

Improving Your Class Standing

Some concepts of classes are given below. Have a look at them:

- Classes have a definite namespace, just like modules. Trying to call a class method from a different class will give you an error unless you qualify it, e.g.

```
spamClass.eggMethod().
```

- Classes support multiple copies. Classes have two different objects: class objects and instance objects. Class objects are used to give the default behavior and are used to create instance objects. Instance objects are the objects that actually do the work in your program. You can have as many instance objects of the same class object as you need.

- Each instance object has its own namespace but also inherits from the base class object. This means each instance has the same default namespace components as the class object, but additionally each instance can make new namespace objects just for itself.

- Classes can define objects that respond to the same operations as built-in types. So, class objects can be sliced, indexed, concatenated, etc. just like strings, lists, and other standard Python types. This is because everything in Python is actually a class object; we aren't actually doing anything new with classes, we're just learning how to better use the inherent nature of the Python language.

So What Does a Class Look Like?

See here you class look like in python:

Defining a class

```
>>> class Item :  #define a classobject

... def setName (self,value) :  #define  class
methods

... self.name = value
#selfidentifiesaparticular instance
```

```
... def display (self) :

... print self.name     #print the data for a particular instance
```

Creating class instances

```
>>> x =  Item ( )

>>> y = Item ( )

>>> z  = Item ( )
```

Adding data to instances

```
>>> x.setName ("Hello, This is Python book.")

>>> y.setName ("I am a quick learner.")
```

```
>>> z.setName ("It is worth buying this
book.")
```

Displaying instance data

```
>>> x.display ( )

Hello, This is Python book.

>>> y.display ( )

I am a quick learner.

>>> z.display ( )

It is worth buying this book.
```

PYTHON DATABASES

In python when you use web applications or customer-oriented programs, Databases are very important. Normal files, such as text files, are easy to create and use; Python has the tools built-in and it doesn't take much to work with files. Databases are used when you work on discrete "structures", such as customer list that has phone numbers, addresses, past orders, etc. database is used to store a lump of data and it allows the user or developer to pull the necessary information, without regard to how the data is stored. Also, databases can be used to retrieve data randomly, rather than sequentially.

How to Use a Database

A database is a collection of data, which is placed into an arbitrary structured format. Most commonly used database is a relational database. In database tables are used to store the data and relationships can be defined between different tables. SQL (Structured Query Language) is the language which is used to work with most Databases. SQL provides the commands to query a database and retrieve or manipulate the information. SQL is also used to input information into a database.

Working With A Database

Database consists of one or more tables, just like a spreadsheet. The vertical columns comprise of different fields or categories; they are analogous to the fields you fill out in a form. The horizontal rows are individual records; each row is one complete record entry. Here is an example representing a customer's list.

USING SQL TO QUERY A DATABASE

Index	LName	FName	Address	City	State
0	Peter	Sam	123 Easy St.	Anywhere	CA
1	Jackson	Harry	312 Hard St.	Somewhere	NY

Here, Index field is the one that provides a unique value to every record; it's often called the primary key field. The primary key is a special object for databases; simply identifying which field is the primary key will automatically increment that field as new entries are made, thereby ensuring a unique data object for easy identification. The other fields are simply created based on the information that you want to include in the database.

Now if you want to make order entry database, and want to link that to the above customer list, so it should be like:

Key	Item_title	Price	Order_Number	Customer_ID
0	Bag	99.5	4455	0
1	Shoes	95	4455	0
2	Purse	50	7690	0
3	Clutch	60.69	3490	1
4	Ring	40	5512	1

This table is called “Orders_table”. This table shows various orders made by each person in the customer table. Each entry has a unique key and is related to Customers_table by the Customer_ID field, which is the Index value for each customer.

Python and SQLite

Python has a SQLite, a light-weight SQL library. SQLite is basically written in C, so it is very quick and easy to understand. It creates the database in a single file, so implementing a database becomes fairly simple; you don't need to worry about the issues of having a database spread across a server. SQLite is good for prototyping your application before you throw in a full-blown database. By this you can easily know how your program works and any problems are most likely with the database implementation. It's also good for small programs that don't need a complete database package with its associated overhead.

Creating an SQLite database

SQLite is built into Python, so it can easily be imported to any other library. Once you import it, you have to make a connection to it; so as to create the database file. Cursor in SQLite performs most of the functions; you will be doing with the database.

```
import sqlite3 #SQLite v3 is the version
currently included with Python

connection = sqlite3.connect
("Hand_tools.database")      #The .
database extension is optional

cursor = connection.cursor ()

#Alternative database created only in
memory

#mem_conn = sqlite3.connect (":memory:")

#cursor = mem_conn.cursor ()

cursor.execute ("""CREATE TABLE Tools (id
INTEGER PRIMARY KEY, name TEXT, size
TEXT, price INTEGER)""")
```

```
for item in ((None,"Book","Small",15),
        #The end comma is required to
separate tuple items
(None,"Purse","Medium",35),(None,"Pen","
Large",55),(None,"
Hat","Small",25),(None,"Handbag","Small",
25),(None,"Socks","Small",10),(None,"Comb
","Large",60),):cursor.execute ("INSERT
INTO Tools VALUES (?,?,?,?)",item)

connection.commit()  #Write data to
database

cursor.close()     #Close database
```

In this example question marks (?) are used to insert items into the table. They are used to prevent a SQL injection attack, where a SQL command is passed to the database as a legitimate value. The question marks act as a substitution value.

Retrieving data from SQLite

To retrieve the data from a SQLite database, you just use the SQL commands that tell the database what information you want and how you want it formatted.

Example:

```
cursor.execute ("SELECT name, size, price
FROM Tools")

tools Tuple = cursor.fetchall ()

for tuple in tools Tuple:name, size, price =
tuple    #unpack the tuples

item = ("%s, %s, %d" % (name, size, price))

print item
```

Output:

```
Book, Small, 15
```

Purse, Medium, 35

Pen, Large, 55

Hat, Small, 25

Handbag, Small, 25

Socks, Small, 10

Comb, Large, 60

Book, Small, 15

Purse, Medium, 35

Pen, Large, 55

Hat, Small, 25

Handbag, Small, 25

Socks, Small, 10

Comb, Large, 60

Dealing With Existing Databases

SQLite will try to recreate the database file every time you run the program. If the database file already exists, you will get an “OperationalError” exception stating that the file already exists. The easiest way to deal with this is to simply catch the exception and ignore it.

```
cursor.execute ("CREATE TABLE Foo (id INTEGER PRIMARY KEY, name TEXT)")

except sqlite3.Operational Error:pass
```

This will allow you to run your database program multiple times without having to delete the database file after every run.

CLASSES

Class is a data structure that is used in python to define objects, which holds data values and behavioral characteristics. Classes are the entities, which are the programs of an abstraction for a problem, and instances are realizations of such objects. The term most likely originates from using classes to identify and categorize biological families of species to which specific creatures belong and can be derived into similar yet distinct subclasses. Many of these features apply to the concept of classes in programming.

In Python, class declarations are similar to the function declarations, a header line with appropriate keyword followed by a suite as its definition, as indicated below:

```
def functionName(args):
'function documentation string'
function_suite
class
ClassName:
'class documentation string'
class_suite
```

Class in python holds multiple data items, and it can also support its own set of functions, which are called methods. You may be asking what other advantages classes have over standard container types such as lists and dictionaries.

Creating Classes

Python classes are created using the class keyword. In the simple form of class declarations, the name of the class immediately follows the keyword:

```
class ClassName:

'class documentation string'

class_suite
```

class_suite consists of all the component statements, defining class members, data attributes, and functions. Classes are generally defined at the top-level of a module so that instances of a class can be created anywhere in a piece of source code where the class is defined.

Class Declaration vs. Definition

In python there is no difference in declaring and defining classes because they occur simultaneously. The definition follows the declaration and the documentation string.

Class Attributes

A class attribute is a functional element, which belongs to another object and is accessed via dotted-attribute notation. In Python, complex numbers have data attributes while lists and dictionaries have functional attributes. When you access attribute, you can also access an object that may have attributes of its own.

For example:

```
- sys.stdout.write('abc')

- print myModule.myClass.__doc__
```

```
- myList.extend(map(upper,
open('x').readlines()))
```

Class attributes are linked to the classes in which they are defined, and instance objects are the most commonly used objects in OOP. Instance data attributes are the primary data attributes that are used. Class data attributes are useful only when a "static" data type is required, which does not require any instances.

Class Data Attributes

Data attributes are the variables of the class which are defined by the programmer. They can be used like any other variable when the class is created and can be updated by methods within the class. These types of attributes are better known to programmers as static members, class variables, or static data. They represent data that is tied to the class object they belong to and are independent of any class instances.

Example of using class data attributes (abc):

```
>>> class C:
... abc = 100
>>> print C.abc
0
>>> C.abc = C.abc + 1
>>> print C.abc
```

Output:

```
101
```

METHODS

In the example given below, MyFirstMethod method of the MyTeam class is simply a function which is defined as part of a class definition. This means that MyMethod applies only to objects or instances of MyTeam type.

For Example:

```
>>> class MyTeam:
def MyFirstMethod(self):
pass
>>> myInstance = MyTeam()
>>> myInstance.MyFirstMethod()
```

Any call to MyFirstMethod by itself as a function fails:

```
>>> MyFirstMethod()
Traceback (innermost last):
File "<stdin>", line 1, in ?
MyFirstMethod()
NameError: MyFirstMethod
```

Here in the above example, NameError exception is raised because there is no such function in the global namespace. Here MyFirstMethod is a method, meaning that it belongs to the class and is not a name in the global namespace. If MyFirstMethod was defined as a function at the top-level, then our call would have succeeded. We show you below that even calling the method with the class object fails.

```
>>> MyTeam.MyFirstMethod()
```

```
Traceback (innermost last):

File "<stdin>", line 1, in ?

MyTeam.MyFirstMethod()

TypeError: unbound method must be called with class instance 1st argument
```

This TypeError exception may seem perplexing at first because you know that the method is an attribute of the class and so are wondering why there is a failure.

Static Methods

Python does not support static methods, and functions which are associated only with a class and not with any particular instances. They are either function, which help manage static class data or are global functions which have some sort of functionality related to the class, in which they are defined. Because python does not support static methods, so a standard global function is required.

INSTANCES

Class is a data structure definition type, while an instance is a declaration of a variable of that type. Or you can say that instances are classes which are brought to life. Instances are the objects which are used primarily during execution, and all instances are of type "instance."

Creating Instances by Invoking Class Object

Most languages provide a new keyword to create an instance of a class. The python's approach is much simpler. Once a class has been defined in python, creating an instance is no more difficult. Using instantiation of the function operator.

For Example:

```
>>> class MyTeam: # define class
```

```
... pass

>>> myInstance = MyTeam() # instantiate class

>>> type(MyTeam) # class is of class type

<type 'class'>

>>> type(myInstance) # instance is of instance type

<type 'instance'>
```

Using the term "type" in Python is different from the instance being of the type of class it was created from. An object's type dictates the behavioral properties of such objects in the Python system, and these types are a subset of all types, which Python supports. User-defined "types" such as classes are categorized in the same manner. Classes share the same type, but have different IDs and values. All classes are defined with the same syntax, so they can be instantiated, and all have the same core properties. Classes are unique objects, which are differ only in definition, hence they are all the same "type" in Python.

Instance Attributes

Instances have only data attributes and these are simply the data values which you want to be associated with a particular instance of any class. They are accessible via the familiar dotted-attribute notation. These values are independent of any other instance or the class it was instantiated from. If any instance is deallocated, then its attributes are also deallocated.

"Instantiating" Instance Attributes

Instance attributes can be set any time after an instance has been created, in any piece of code that has access to the instance. However, one of the key places where such attributes are set is in the constructor, __init__ ().

Constructor First Place to Set Instance Attributes

The constructor is the earliest place that instance attributes can be set because __init__ () is the first method called after instance objects have been created. There is no earlier opportunity to set instance attributes. Once __init__ () has finished execution, the instance object is returned, completing the instantiation process.

Default Arguments Provide Default Instance Setup

One can also use __init__ () along with default arguments to provide an effective way in preparing an instance for use. In most of the cases, the default values represent the most common cases for setting up instance attributes, and such use of default values precludes them from having to be given explicitly to the constructor.

Built-in Type Attributes

Built-in types also have attributes, and although they are technically not class instance attributes, they are sufficiently similar to get a brief mention here. Type attributes do not have an attribute dictionary like classes and instances (__dict__), so how do we figure out what attributes built-in types have? The convention for built-in types is to use two special attributes, __methods__ and __members__, to outline any methods and/or data attributes.

Instance Attributes vs. Class Attributes

Class attributes are simply data values which are associated with a class and with not any particular instances. Such values are also referred to as static members because their values remain constant, even if a class is invoked due to instantiation multiple times. No matter what, static members maintain their values independent of instances unless explicitly changed. Comparing instance attributes to class attributes is just similar to comparing automatic and static variables. Their main aspect is that you can access a class attribute with either the class or an instance, while the instance does not have an attribute with the same name.

Python Database Access

The standard database used for Python is DB-API. Most Python database interfaces adhere to this standard. You can choose the right database for your application. Python Database API supports a wide range of database servers such as, GadFly, mSQL, MySQL, PostgreSQL, Microsoft SQL Server 11000, Informix, Interbase, Oracle, Sybase. You must download a separate DB API module for each database that you need to access. For example, if you need to access an Oracle database as well as a MySQL database, then you need to download both the Oracle and the MySQL database modules.

The DB API provides a minimal standard for working with databases using Python structures and syntax wherever possible.

The API includes:

- Importing the API module.
- Acquiring a connection with the database.
- Issuing SQL statements and stored procedures.
- Closing the connection

We would learn all the concepts using MySQL, so let's talk about MySQLdb module only.

What is MySQLdb?

MySQLdb is an interface for connecting to a MySQL database server from Python. It implements the Python Database API v2.0 and is built on top of the MySQL C API.

How to install MySQLdb?

Before proceeding, you make sure you have MySQLdb installed on your Tomhine. Just type the following in your Python script and execute it:

```
#!/usr/bin/python

import MySQLdb
```

If it produces the following result, then it means MySQLdb module is not installed:

```
Traceback (most recent call last):

File "test.py", line 3, in <module>

import MySQLdb

ImportError: No module named MySQLdb
```

To install MySQLdb module, download it from MySQLdb Download page and proceed as follows:

```
$ gunzip MySQL-python-1.2.2.tar.gz

$ tar -xvf MySQL-python-1.2.2.tar

$ cd MySQL-python-1.2.2

$ python setup.py build

$ python setup.py install
```

Database Connection:

Before connecting to a MySQL database, you need to make sure of the followings points given below:

- You have created a database TESTDB.
- You have created a table STAFF in TESTDB.
- This table is having fields FIRST_NAME, LAST_NAME, AGE, SEX and INCOME.
- User ID "abctest" and password "python121" are set to access TESTDB.

• Python module MySQLdb is installed properly on your Tomhine.

• You have gone through MySQL tutorial to understand MySQL Basics.

For Example:

Connecting with MySQL database "TESTDB":

```
#!/usr/bin/python

import MySQLdb

# Open database connection

db =
MySQLdb.connect("localhost","abctest","py
thon121","TESTDB")

# prepare a cursor object using cursor()
method

cursor = db.cursor()
```

```
# execute SQL query using execute()
method.

cursor.execute("SELECT VERSION()")

# Fetch a single row using fetchone()
method.

data = cursor.fetchone()

print "Database version : %s " % data

# disconnect from server

db.close()
```

Output:

```
Database version : 5.0.45
```

Creating Database Table:

Once a database connection is established, you can easily create tables or records into the database using execute method.

Example for creating Database table STAFF:

```
#!/usr/bin/python

import MySQLdb

# Open database connection

db =
MySQLdb.connect("localhost","abctest","py
thon121","TESTDB")

# prepare a cursor object using cursor()
method

cursor = db.cursor()

# Drop table if it already exist using
execute() method.

cursor.execute("DROP TABLE IF EXISTS
STAFF")
```

```
# Create table as per requirement sql =
"""CREATE TABLE STAFF (FIRST_NAME
CHAR(20) NOT NULL,LAST_NAME
CHAR(20),AGE INT,SEX CHAR(1),INCOME
FLOAT )"""

cursor.execute(sql)

# disconnect from server

db.close()
```

INSERT Operation:

INSERT operation is required when you want to create your records into a database table.

Example to create a record into STAFF table:

```
#!/usr/bin/python

import MySQLdb
```

```
# Open database connection

db =
MySQLdb.connect("localhost","abctest","py
thon121","TESTDB" )

# prepare a cursor object using cursor()
method

cursor = db.cursor()

# Prepare SQL query to INSERT a record into
the database.

sql = """INSERT INTO
STAFF(FIRST_NAME,LAST_NAME, AGE, SEX,
INCOME)

VALUES ('Tom', 'David', 20, 'M', 11000)"""

try:

# Execute the SQL command

cursor.execute(sql)

# Commit your changes in the database

db.commit()
```

```
except:
# Rollback in case there is any error
db.rollback()
# disconnect from server
db.close()
```

Above example can be written as follows to create SQL queries dynamically:

```
#!/usr/bin/python
import MySQLdb
# Open database connection
db =
MySQLdb.connect("localhost","abctest","py
thon121","TESTDB" )
# prepare a cursor object using cursor()
method
cursor = db.cursor()
```

```
# Prepare SQL query to INSERT a record into the database.

sql = "INSERT INTO STAFF(FIRST_NAME, \LAST_NAME, AGE, SEX, INCOME) \

VALUES ('%s', '%s', '%d', '%c', '%d' )" % \ ('Tom', 'David', 20, 'M', 11000)

try:

# Execute the SQL command

cursor.execute(sql)

# Commit your changes in the database

db.commit()

except:

# Rollback in case there is any error

db.rollback()

# disconnect from server

db.close()
```

READ Operation:

READ Operation on database means to fetch some useful information from the database. Once our database connection is established, we are ready to make a query into this database. We can use either fetchone() method to fetch single record or fetchall() method to fetech multiple values from a database table.

- **fetchone():** This method fetches the next row of a query result set. A result set is an object that is returned when a cursor object is used to query a table.

- **fetchall():** This method fetches all the rows in a result set. If some rows have already been extracted from the result set, the fetchall() method retrieves the remaining rows from the result set.

• **rowcount:** This is a read-only attribute and returns the number of rows that were affected by an execute() method.

Example to query all the records from STAFF table having salary more than 5000:

```
#!/usr/bin/python

import MySQLdb

# Open database connection

db =
MySQLdb.connect("localhost","abctest","py
thon121","TESTDB" )

# prepare a cursor object using cursor()
method

cursor = db.cursor()

# Prepare SQL query to INSERT a record into
the database.

sql = "SELECT * FROM STAFF \
```

```
WHERE INCOME > '%d'" % (1000)

try:

# Execute the SQL command

cursor.execute(sql)

# Fetch all the rows in a list of lists.

results = cursor.fetchall()

for row in results:

fname = row[0]

lname = row[1]

age = row[2]

sex = row[3]

income = row[4]

# Now print fetched result

print
"fname=%s,lname=%s,age=%d,sex=%s,inco
me=%d" % \
```

```
(fname, lname, age, sex, income )

except:

print "Error: unable to fecth data"

# disconnect from server

db.close()
```

Output:

```
fname=Tom, lname=David, age=20, sex=M,
income=11000
```

Update Operation:

UPDATE Operation on any database means to update one or more records, which are already available in the database. Following is the procedure to update all the records having SEX as 'M'. Here, we will increase AGE of all the males by one year.

For Example:

```
#!/usr/bin/python

import MySQLdb

# Open database connection

db =
MySQLdb.connect("localhost","abctest","py
thon121","TESTDB" )

# prepare a cursor object using cursor()
method

cursor = db.cursor()

# Prepare SQL query to UPDATE required
records

sql = "UPDATE STAFF SET AGE = AGE + 1

WHERE SEX = '%c'" % ('M')

try:

# Execute the SQL command

cursor.execute(sql)
```

```
# Commit your changes in the database

db.commit()

except:

# Rollback in case there is any error

db.rollback()

# disconnect from server

db.close()
```

DELETE Operation:

DELETE operation is required when you want to delete some records from your database. Following is the procedure to delete all the records from STAFF where AGE is more than 20:

For Example:

```
#!/usr/bin/python
```

```
import MySQLdb

# Open database connection

db =
MySQLdb.connect("localhost","abctest","py
thon121","TESTDB" )

# prepare a cursor object using cursor()
method

cursor = db.cursor()

# Prepare SQL query to DELETE required
records

sql = "DELETE FROM STAFF WHERE AGE >
'%d'" % (20)

try:

# Execute the SQL command

cursor.execute(sql)

# Commit your changes in the database

db.commit()
```

```
except:
# Rollback in case there is any error
db.rollback()
# disconnect from server
db.close()
```

Performing Transactions:

Transactions are a mechanism that ensures consistency of data. Transactions should have the following properties:

- **Atomicity**: Either a transaction completes or nothing happens at all.
- **Consistency**: A transaction must start in a consistent state and leave the system in a consistent state.

• **Isolation**: Intermediate results of a transaction are not visible outside the current transaction.

• **Durability**: Once a transaction was committed, the effects are persistent, even after a system failure.

The Python DB API 2.0 provides two methods to either commit or rollback a transaction.

For Example:

```
# Prepare SQL query to DELETE required records

sql = "DELETE FROM STAFF WHERE AGE > '%d'" % (20)

try:

# Execute the SQL command

cursor.execute(sql)
```

```
# Commit your changes in the database
db.commit()
except:
# Rollback in case there is any error
db.rollback()
```

COMMIT Operation:

Commit is the operation, which gives a green signal to database to finalize the changes, and after this operation, no change can be reverted back.

For Example:

```
db.commit()
```

ROLLBACK Operation:

If you are not satisfied with one or more of the changes and you want to revert back those changes completely, then use rollback() method.

For Example:

```
db.rollback()
```

Disconnecting Database:

To disconnect Database connection, use close() method.

For Example:

```
db.close()
```

If the connection to a database is closed by the user with the close() method, any outstanding transactions are rolled back by the DB. However, instead of depending on any of DB lower level implementation details, your application would be better off calling commit or rollback explicitly.

Handling Errors:

There are many sources of errors. A few examples are a syntax error in an executed SQL statement, a connection failure, or calling the fetch method for an already canceled or finished statement handle. The DB API defines a number of errors that must exist in each database module. The following table lists these exceptions.

Exception Description

Warning Used for non-fatal issues. Must subclass StandardError.

Error Base class for errors. Must subclass StandardError.

InterfaceError

Used for errors in the database module, not the database itself. Must subclass Error.

DatabaseError

Used for errors in the database. Must subclass Error. DataError Subclass of DatabaseError that refers to errors in the data.

OperationalError

Subclass of DatabaseError that refers to errors such as the loss of a connection to the database. These errors are generally outside of the control of the Python scripter.

IntegrityError

Subclass of DatabaseError for situations that would damage the relational integrity, such as uniqueness constraints or foreign keys.

InternalError

Subclass of DatabaseError that refers to errors internal to the database module, such as a cursor no longer being active.

ProgrammingError

Subclass of DatabaseError that refers to errors such as a bad table name and other things that can safely be blamed on you.

NotSupportedError

Subclass of DatabaseError that refers to trying to call unsupported functionality.

Your Python scripts should handle these errors, but before using any of the above exceptions, make sure your MySQLdb has support for that exception. You can get more information about them by reading the DB API 2.0 specification.

PYTHON NETWORKING

Python provides two levels of access to network services. At a low level, you can access the basic socket support in the underlying operating system which allows you to implement clients and servers for both connection oriented and connectionless protocols. Python also has libraries that provide higher-level access to specific application-level network protocols, such as FTP, HTTP, and so on.

What are Sockets?

Sockets are the endpoints of a bidirectional communications channel. Sockets may communicate within a process, between processes on the same machine, or between processes on different continents. Sockets may be implemented over a number of different channel types: UNIX domain sockets, TCP, UDP, and so on. The socket library provides specific classes for handling the common transports as well as a generic interface for handling the rest.

Sockets have their own vocabulary:

Term	Description
domain	The family of protocols that will be used as the transport mechanism. These values are constants such as AF_INET, PF_INET, PF_UNIX, PF_X25, and so on.
type	The type of communications between the two endpoints, typically SOCK_STREAM for connection-oriented protocols and SOCK_DGRAM for connectionless protocols.
protocol	Typically zero, this may be used to identify a variant of a protocol within a domain and type.
hostname	The identifier of a network interface:
	• A string, which can be a host name, a dotted-quad address, or an IPV6 address in colon (and possibly dot) notation
	• A string "<broadcast>", which specifies an INADDR_BROADCAST address.
	• A zero-length string, which specifies INADDR_ANY, or
	• An Integer, interpreted as a binary address in host byte order.
port	Each server listens for clients calling on one or more ports. A port may be a Fixnum port number, a string containing a port number, or the name of a service.

The socket Module:

To create a socket, you must use the socket.socket() function available in socket module. Syntax:

s = socket.socket (socket_family, socket_type, protocol=0)

Description of parameters:

• **socket_family**: This is either AF_UNIX or AF_INET, as explained earlier.

• **socket_type**: This is either SOCK_STREAM or SOCK_DGRAM.

• **protocol**: This is usually left out, defaulting to 0.

Socket objects are use required functions to create your client or server program. Here I am going to share with you the list of functions required:

Server Socket Methods:

Method	Description
s.bind()	This method binds address (hostname, port number pair) to socket.
s.listen()	This method sets up and start TCP listener.
s.accept()	This passively accepts TCP client connection, waiting until connection arrives (blocking).

Client Socket Methods:

Method	Description
s.connect()	This method actively initiates TCP server connection.

General Socket Methods:

Method	Description
s.recv()	This method receives TCP message
s.send()	This method transmits TCP message
s.recvfrom()	This method receives UDP message
s.sendto()	This method transmits UDP message
s.close()	This method closes socket
socket.gethostname()	Returns the hostname

A Simple Server:

To write Internet servers, we use the socket function available in socket module to create a socket object. A socket object is then used to call other functions to set up a socket server. Now, call bind (hostname, port) function to specify a port for your service on the given host.

Next, call the accept method of the returned object. This method waits until a client connects to the port you specified and then returns a connection object that represents the connection to that client.

Example:

```
#!/usr/bin/python # This is server.py file

import socket # Import socket module

s = socket.socket() # Create a socket object
```

```
host = socket.gethostname() # Get local
machine name

port = 102 # Reserve a port for your service.

s.bind((host, port)) # Bind to the port

s.listen(5) # Now wait for client connection.

while True:

c, addr = s.accept() # Establish connection
with client.

print 'Got connection from', addr

c.send('Thanks for connecting')

c.close() # Close the connection
```

A Simple Client:

Now, we will write a very simple client program, which will open a connection to a given port 102 and given host. This is very simple to create a socket client using Python's socket module function. The socket.connect(hosname, port) opens a TCP connection to hostname on the port. Once you have a socket open, you can read from it like any IO object. When done, remember to close it, as you would close a file. The following code is a very simple client that connects to a given host and port, reads any available data from the socket, and then exits:

Example:

```
#!/usr/bin/python # This is client.py file

import socket # Import socket module

s = socket.socket() # Create a socket object

host = socket.gethostname() # Get local machine name

port = 102 # Reserve a port for your service.

s.connect((host, port))
```

```
print s.recv(1024)
s.close # Close the socket when done
```

Now, run this server.py in background and then run above client.py to see the result.

```
# Following would start a server in background.
$ python server.py &
# Once server is started run client as follows:
$ python client.py
```

Output:

```
Got connection from ('127.0.0.1', 48437)
Thanks for connecting
```

Python Internet modules

Here below is a list of some important modules, which are used in Python Network/Internet programming.

Protocol	Common function	Port No	Python module
HTTP	Web pages	80	httplib, urllib, xmlrpclib
NNTP	Usenet news	119	nntplib
FTP	File transfers	20	ftplib, urllib
SMTP	Sending email	25	smtplib
POP3	Fetching email	110	poplib
IMAP4	Fetching email	143	imaplib
Telnet	Command lines	23	telnetlib
Gopher	Document transfers	70	gopherlib, urllib

SENDING MAIL IN PYTHON

Simple Mail Transfer Protocol (SMTP) is a protocol that is used to send e-mails and routing e-mails between the mail servers. In Python there is 'smtplib' module, which defines an SMTP client session object. SMTP client session object is used to send mail to any Internet machine with an SMTP or ESMTP listener daemon.

SYNTAX:

```
import smtplib

smtpObj =
smtplib.SMTP([host[,port[,local_hostname]]
])
```

Detail of parameters used:

• **host**: This is the host running your SMTP server. You can specify IP address of the host or a domain name. This is optional argument.

• **port**: If you are providing host argument, then you need to specify a port, where SMTP server is listening. Usually this port would be 25.

• **local_hostname**: If your SMTP server is running on your local machine, then you can specify justlocalhost as of this option. An SMTP object has an instance method called sendmail, which will typically be used to do the work of mailing a message. It takes three parameters:

• **The sender** - A string with the address of the sender.

• **The receivers** - A list of strings, one for each recipient.

• **The message** - A message as a string formatted as specified in the various RFCs.

Example:

To send an e-mail using Python script.

```
#!/usr/bin/python

import smtplib

sender = 'abc@senddomain.com'

receivers = ['xyz@recdomain.com']

message = """From: From Person
<abc@senddomain.com>

To: To Person <xyz@recdomain.com>

Subject: SMTP e-mail test

This is a test e-mail message.

"""

try:

smtpObj = smtplib.SMTP('localhost')

smtpObj.sendmail(sender, receivers,
message)
```

```
print "Mail sent successfully"
except SMTPException:
print "Error in sending mail"
```

In case, if you are not running an SMTP server on your local machine, then you can use 'smtplib' client to communicate with a remote SMTP server. Unless you're using a webmail service, your e-mail provider will have provided you with outgoing mail server details that you can provide them, as follows:

```
smtplib.SMTP('mail.your-domain.com', 25)
```

Sending an HTML E-mails Using Python:

When you send a text message using Python, then all the content will be treated as simple text. Even if you will include HTML tags in a text message, it will be displayed as simple text and HTML tags will not be formatted according to HTML syntax. But Python provides option to send an HTML message as actual HTML message. While sending an e-mail message, you can specify a Mime version, content type and character set to send an HTML e-mail.

Example to send HTML content as an e-mail:

```
#!/usr/bin/python

import smtplib

message = """From: From Person
<abc@senddomain.com>

To: To Person <xyz@recdomain.com>

MIME-Version: 1.0

Content-type: text/html
```

```
Subject: SMTP HTML e-mail test

This is an e-mail message to be sent in HTML format

<b>Here is HTML text for you.</b>

<h1>Here is Headline for you.</h1>

"""

try:

smtpObj = smtplib.SMTP('localhost')

smtpObj.sendmail(sender, receivers, message)

print "Mail sent successfully"

except SMTPException:

print "Error in sending mail"
```

Sending Attachments as an e-mail:

To send an e-mail with mixed content requires setting Content-type header to multipart/mixed. Then, text and attachment sections can be specified within boundaries. A boundary is started with two hyphens followed by a unique number, which can not appear in the message part of the e-mail. A final boundary denoting the e-mail's final section must also end with two hyphens. Attached files should be encoded with the pack("m") function to have base64 encoding before transmission.

Example to send a file /tmp/test.txt as an attachment:

```
#!/usr/bin/python

import smtplib

import base64

filename = "/tmp/test.txt"
```

```
# Read a file and encode it into base64 format

fo = open(filename, "rb")

filecontent = fo.read()

encodedcontent = base64.b64encode(filecontent) # base64

sender = 'test@aaadomain.com'

reciever = 'aaa.admin@gmail.com'

marker = "TESTMARKER"

body ="""

This is a test email to send an attachement.

"""

# Define the main headers.

part1 = """From: From Person <me@fromdomain.net>

To: To Person <aaa.admin@gmail.com>

Subject: Sending Attachement
```

```
MIME-Version: 1.0

Content-Type: multipart/mixed;
boundary=%s

--%s

""" % (marker, marker)

# Define the message action

part2 = """Content-Type: text/plain

Content-Transfer-Encoding:8bit

%s

--%s

""" % (body,marker)

# Define the attachment section

part3 = """Content-Type: multipart/mixed;
name=\"%s\"

Content-Transfer-Encoding:base64

Content-Disposition: attachment;
filename=%s
```

```
%s

--%s--

""" %(filename, filename, encodedcontent, marker)

message = part1 + part2 + part3

try:

smtpObj = smtplib.SMTP('localhost')

smtpObj.sendmail(sender, reciever, message)

print "Mail sent successfully"

except Exception:

print "Error in sending email"
```

PYTHON MULTITHREADING

In python you can run multiple threads at a time. Running multiple threads is similar to running several different programs with following benefits:

- Multiple threads within a process share the same data space with the main thread and can share information or communicate with each other more easily as compared to when they were separate processes.
- Threads sometimes called light-weight processes and they don't require much memory overhead. A thread has a beginning, an execution sequence, and a conclusion. It has an instruction pointer that keeps track of where within its context it is currently running.

- It can be pre-empted.
- It can temporarily be put on hold while other threads are running, this method is called yielding.

Starting a New Thread:

To start a new thread, you need to call following method available in thread module:

```
thread.start_new_thread (function, args[,kwargs])
```

This method is used to enable a fast and efficient way to create new threads in both Linux and Windows. The method call returns immediately and the child thread starts and calls function with the passed list of 'agrs'. When function returns, then the thread terminates. Here, 'args' is a tuple of arguments; that uses an empty tuple to call function without passing any arguments. 'kwargs' is an optional dictionary of keyword arguments.

For Example:

```
#!/usr/bin/python

import thread

import time

# Define a function for the thread

def print_time( threadName, delay):

count = 0

while count < 5:

time.sleep(delay)

count += 1
```

```
print "%s: %s" % ( threadName, time.ctime(time.time()) )

# Create two threads as follows

try:

thread.start_new_thread( print_time, ("MyThread-1", 2,) )

thread.start_new_thread( print_time, ("MyThread-2", 4,) )

except:

print "Error in starting a thread"

while 1:

pass
```

Output:

```
MyThread-1: Wed Jan 01:45 01:45:17 2015

MyThread-1: Wed Jan 01:45 01:45:19 2015

MyThread-2: Wed Jan 01:45 01:45:19 2015
```

```
MyThread-1: Wed Jan 01:45 01:45:21 2015
MyThread-2: Wed Jan 01:45 01:45:23 2015
MyThread-1: Wed Jan 01:45 01:45:23 2015
MyThread-1: Wed Jan 01:45 01:45:25 2015
MyThread-2: Wed Jan 01:45 01:45:27 2015
MyThread-2: Wed Jan 01:45 01:45:31 2015
MyThread-2: Wed Jan 01:45 01:45:35 2015
```

Although it is very effective for low-level threading, but the thread module is very limited compared to the newer threading module.

The Threading Module:

New threading module in Python 2.4 provides much more powerful, high-level support for threads. The threading module exposes all the methods of the thread module and provides some additional methods:

- threading.activeCount(): Returns the number of thread objects that are active.
- threading.currentThread(): Returns the number of thread objects in the caller's thread control.
- threading.enumerate(): Returns a list of all thread objects that are currently active.

In addition to the methods, the threading module has the Thread class that implements threading. The methods provided by the Thread class are given below:

- **run()**: The run() method is the entry point for a thread.
- **start()**: The start() method starts a thread by calling the run method.

- **join([time])**: The join() waits for threads to terminate.
- **isAlive()**: The isAlive() method checks whether a thread is still executing.
- **getName()**: The getName() method returns the name of a thread.
- **setName()**: The setName() method sets the name of a thread.

Creating Thread using Threading Module:

To implement a new thread using the threading module, you must follow the points given below:

- Define a new subclass of the Thread class.
- Override the __init__(self [,args]) method to add additional arguments.

• Then, override the run(self [,args]) method to implement what the thread should do when started.

Once you have created the new Thread subclass, you can create an instance of it and then start a new thread by invoking the start(), which will in turn call run() method.

For Example:

```
#!/usr/bin/python

import threading

import time

exitFlag = 0

class myBook (threading.Thread):

def __init__(self, threadID, name, counter):

threading.Thread.__init__(self)
```

```
self.threadID = threadID

self.name = name

self.counter = counter

def run(self):

print "Starting " + self.name

print_time(self.name, self.counter, 5)

print "Exiting " + self.name

def print_time(threadName, delay,
counter):

while counter:

if exitFlag:

thread.exit()

time.sleep(delay)

print "%s: %s" % (threadName,
time.ctime(time.time()))

counter -= 1
```

```
# Create new threads

thread1 = myBook(1, "MyThread-1", 1)

thread2 = myBook(2, "MyThread-2", 2)

# Start new Threads

thread1.start()

thread2.start()

print "Exit From Main Thread"
```

Output:

```
Starting MyThread-1

Starting MyThread-2

Exit From Main Thread

MyThread-1: Mon Jul 27 01:45:10:03 2015

MyThread-1: Mon Jul 27 01:45:10:04 2015

MyThread-2: Mon Jul 27 01:45:10:04 2015
```

```
MyThread-1: Mon Jul 27 01:45:10:05 2015

MyThread-1: Mon Jul 27 01:45:10:06 2015

MyThread-2: Mon Jul 27 01:45:10:06 2015

MyThread-1: Mon Jul 27 01:45:10:07 2015

Exiting MyThread-1

MyThread-2: Mon Jul 27 01:45:10:08 2015

MyThread-2: Mon Jul 27 01:45:10:10 2015

MyThread-2: Mon Jul 27 01:45:10:12 2015

Exiting MyThread-2
```

Synchronizing Threads:

In python threading module includes a simple-to-implement locking mechanism which will allow you to synchronize the threads. A new lock is created by calling the Lock() method, which returns the new lock.

to force threads to run, The acquire(blocking) method of the new lock object is used. If blocking is set to 0, the thread will return immediately with a 0 value if the lock cannot be acquired and with a 1 if the lock was acquired. If blocking is set to 1, the thread will block and wait for the lock to be released. The release() method of the new lock object would be used to release the lock when it is no longer required.

For Example:

```
#!/usr/bin/python

import threading

import time

class myBook (threading.Thread):

def __init__(self, threadID, name, counter):

threading.Thread.__init__(self)
```

```
self.threadID = threadID

self.name = name

self.counter = counter

def run(self):

print "Starting " + self.name

# Get lock to synchronize threads

threadLock.acquire()

print_time(self.name, self.counter, 3)

# Free lock to release next thread

threadLock.release()

def print_time(threadName, delay,
counter):

while counter:

time.sleep(delay)

print "%s: %s" % (threadName,
time.ctime(time.time()))
```

```
counter -= 1
threadLock = threading.Lock()
threads = []
# Create new threads
thread1 = myBook(1, "MyThread-1", 1)
thread2 = myBook(2, "MyThread-2", 2)
# Start new Threads
thread1.start()
thread2.start()
# Add threads to thread list
threads.append(thread1)
threads.append(thread2)
# Wait for all threads to complete
for t in threads:
t.join()
```

```
print "Exiting from Main Thread"
```

Output:

```
Starting MyThread-2
MyThread-1: Mon Jul 27 01:45:11:28 2015
MyThread-1: Mon Jul 27 01:45:11:29 2015
MyThread-1: Mon Jul 27 01:45:11:30 2015
MyThread-2: Mon Jul 27 01:45:11:32 2015
MyThread-2: Mon Jul 27 01:45:11:34 2015
MyThread-2: Mon Jul 27 01:45:11:36 2015
Exiting from Main Thread
```

Multithreaded Priority Queue:

The Queue module in python allows you to create a new queue object, which can hold a specific number of items. Methods that are used to control the Queue are given below:

- **get()**: The get() removes and returns an item from the queue.
- **put()**: The put adds item to a queue.
- **qsize()** : The qsize() returns the number of items that are currently in the queue.
- **empty()**: The empty( ) returns True if queue is empty; otherwise, False.
- **full()**: the full() returns True if queue is full; otherwise, False.

For Example:

```
#!/usr/bin/python
```

```
import Queue
import threading
import time
exitFlag = 0
class myBook (threading.Thread):
def __init__(self, threadID, name, q):
threading.Thread.__init__(self)
self.threadID = threadID
self.name = name
self.q = q
def run(self):
print "Starting " + self.name
process_data(self.name, self.q)
print "Exiting " + self.name
def process_data(threadName, q):
```

```
while not exitFlag:

queueLock.acquire()

if not workQueue.empty():

data = q.get()

queueLock.release()

print "%s processing %s" % (threadName,
data)

else:

queueLock.release()

time.sleep(1)

threadList = ["MyThread-1", "MyThread-2",
"Thread-3"]

nameList = ["A", "B", "C", "D", "E"]

queueLock = threading.Lock()

workQueue = Queue.Queue(10)

threads = []
```

```
threadID = 1

# Create new threads

for tName in threadList:

thread = myThread(threadID, tName,
workQueue)

thread.start()

threads.append(thread)

threadID += 1

# Fill the queue

queueLock.acquire()

for word in nameList:

workQueue.put(word)

queueLock.release()

# Wait for queue to empty

while not workQueue.empty():

pass
```

```
# Notify threads it's time to exit
exitFlag = 1
# Wait for all threads to complete
for t in threads:
t.join()
print "Exiting Main Thread"
```

Output:

```
Starting Thread-1
Starting Thread-2
Starting Thread-3
Thread-1 processing A
Thread-2 processing B
Thread-3 processing C
Thread-1 processing D
```

Thread-2 processing E

Exiting Thread-3

Exiting Thread-1

Exiting Thread-2

Exiting Main Thread

PYTHON XML PROCESSING

What is XML?

XML is, Extensible Markup Language (XML) and it's like HTML or SGML. XML is a portable, open source language that allows the programmers to develop applications that can be read by other applications, regardless of operating system and/or developmental language. XML is extremely useful for keeping track of small to medium amounts of data.

XML Parser Architectures and APIs:

The Python standard library provides a set of interfaces to work with XML. The two most basic and broadly used

APIs to XML data are the SAX and DOM interfaces.

• **Simple API for XML (SAX):** Here, you register callbacks for events of interest and then let the parser proceed through the document. This is useful when your documents are large or you have memory limitations, it parses the file as it reads it from disk and the entire file is never stored in memory.

• **Document Object Model (DOM) API:** This is a World Wide Web Consortium recommendation wherein the entire file is read into memory and stored in a hierarchical (tree-based) form to represent all the features of an XML document.

The thing is that SAX can't process information as fast as DOM, when working with large files. On the other hand, using DOM can kill your resources, especially if used on a lot of small files. SAX is read-only, while DOM allows changes to the XML file. As these two APIs complement each other, there is no reason why you can't use them both for large projects. Let's see a simple example for XML file movies.xml:

```
<collection shelf="New Arrivals">

<movie title="Enemy Behind">

<type>War, Thriller</type>

<format>DVD</format>

<year>2003</year>

<rating>PG</rating>

<stars>10</stars>

<description>Talk about a US-Japan
war</description>

</movie>

<movie title="Transformers">

<type>Anime, Science Fiction</type>
```

```
<format>DVD</format>

<year>1989</year>

<rating>R</rating>

<stars>8</stars>

<description>A schientific
fiction</description>

</movie>

<movie title="Trigun">

<type>Anime, Action</type>

<format>DVD</format>

<episodes>4</episodes>

<rating>PG</rating>

<stars>10</stars>

<description>Vash the
Stampede!</description>

</movie>
```

```
<movie title="Ishtar">

<type>Comedy</type>

<format>VHS</format>

<rating>PG</rating>

<stars>2</stars>

<description>Viewable
boredom</description>

</movie>

</collection>
```

Parsing XML with SAX APIs:

SAX is a standard interface for event-driven XML parsing. For Parsing XML with SAX, you need to create your own ContentHandler by subclassing xml.sax.ContentHandler. Your ContentHandler handles the particular tags and attributes of your flavor of XML. A ContentHandler object provides methods to handle various parsing events. Its owning parser calls ContentHandler methods as it passes the XML file. The methods startDocument and endDocument are called at the start and the end of the XML file. The ContentHandler is called at the start and end of each element. Here are some methods to understand before proceeding:

The make_parser Method:

This method creates a new parser object and returns it. The parser object created will be of the first parser type the system finds.

```
xml.sax.make_parser( [parser_list] )
```

Here parameter 'parser_list', is the optional argument consisting of a list of parsers to use which must all implement the make_parser method.

The parse Method:

This method creates a SAX parser and uses it to parse a document.

```
xml.sax.parse( xmlfile, contenthandler[,
errorhandler])
```

Here parameters 'xmlfile', is the name of the XML file to read from. 'contenthandler', must be a ContentHandler object. and 'errorhandler', must be a SAX ErrorHandler object.

The parseString Method:

There is one more method to create a SAX parser and to parse the specified XML string.

```
xml.sax.parseString(xmlstring,
contenthandler[, errorhandler])
```

Here parameters 'xmlstring', is the name of the XML string to read from. 'contenthandler', must be a ContentHandler object. 'errorhandler', must be a SAX ErrorHandler object.

For Example:

```
#!/usr/bin/python

import xml.sax

class MovieHandler(
xml.sax.ContentHandler ):

def __init__(self):

self.CurrentData = ""

self.type = ""

self.format = ""
```

```
self.year = ""
self.rating = ""
self.stars = ""
self.description = ""
# Call when an element starts
def startElement(self, tag, attributes):
self.CurrentData = tag
if tag == "movie":
print "*****Movie*****"
title = attributes["title"]
print "Title:", title
# Call when an elements ends
def endElement(self, tag):
if self.CurrentData == "type":
print "Type:", self.type
```

```
elif self.CurrentData == "format":
print "Format:", self.format
elif self.CurrentData == "year":
print "Year:", self.year
elif self.CurrentData == "rating":
print "Rating:", self.rating
elif self.CurrentData == "stars":
print "Stars:", self.stars
elif self.CurrentData == "description":
print "Description:", self.description
self.CurrentData = ""
# Call when a character is read
def characters(self, content):
if self.CurrentData == "type":
self.type = content
```

```
elif self.CurrentData == "format":
self.format = content
elif self.CurrentData == "year":
self.year = content
elif self.CurrentData == "rating":
self.rating = content
elif self.CurrentData == "stars":
self.stars = content
elif self.CurrentData == "description":
self.description = content
if ( __name__ == "__main__"):
# create an XMLReader
parser = xml.sax.make_parser()
# turn off namepsaces
parser.setFeature(xml.sax.handler.feature_
namespaces, 0)
```

```
# override the default ContextHandler
Handler = MovieHandler()
parser.setContentHandler( Handler )
parser.parse("movies.xml")
```

Output:

```
*****Movie*****
Title: Enemy Behind
Type: War, Thriller
Format: DVD
Year: 2003
Rating: PG
Stars: 10
Description: Talk about a US-Japan war
*****Movie*****
```

Title: Transformers

Type: Anime, Science Fiction

Format: DVD

Year: 1989

Rating: R

Stars: 8

Description: A schientific fiction

*****Movie*****

Title: Trigun

Type: Anime, Action

Format: DVD

Rating: PG

Stars: 10

Description: Vash the Stampede!

*****Movie*****

Title: Ishtar

Type: Comedy

Format: VHS

Rating: PG

Stars: 2

Description: Viewable boredom

Parsing XML with DOM APIs:

The Document Object Model or "DOM," is a cross-language API which is used for accessing and modifying the XML documents. The DOM is extremely useful for random-access applications. SAX allows to use one document at a time. If you are looking at one SAX element, you have no access to another one. the easiest way to quickly load an XML document and to create a minidom object is by using the xml.dom module. The minidom object provides a simple parser method that will quickly create a DOM tree from the XML file.

For Example:

```
#!/usr/bin/python

from xml.dom.minidom import parse

import xml.dom.minidom

# Open XML document using minidom
parser

DOMTree =
xml.dom.minidom.parse("movies.xml")

collection = DOMTree.documentElement

if collection.hasAttribute("shelf"):

print "Root element : %s" %
collection.getAttribute("shelf")

# Get all the movies in the collection
```

```
movies =
collection.getElementsByTagName("movie"
)

# Print detail of each movie.

for movie in movies:

print "*****Movie*****"

if movie.hasAttribute("title"):

print "Title: %s" %
movie.getAttribute("title")

type =
movie.getElementsByTagName('type')[0]

print "Type: %s" % type.childNodes[0].data

format =
movie.getElementsByTagName('format')[0]

print "Format: %s" %
format.childNodes[0].data

rating =
movie.getElementsByTagName('rating')[0]
```

```
print "Rating: %s" %
rating.childNodes[0].data

description =
movie.getElementsByTagName('description'
)[0]

print "Description: %s" %
description.childNodes[0].data
```

Output:

```
Root element : New Arrivals

*****Movie*****

Title: Enemy Behind

Type: War, Thriller

Format: DVD

Rating: PG

Description: Talk about a US-Japan war

*****Movie*****
```

Title: Transformers

Type: Anime, Science Fiction

Format: DVD

Rating: R

Description: A schientific fiction

*****Movie*****

Title: Trigun

Type: Anime, Action

Format: DVD

Rating: PG

Description: Vash the Stampede!

*****Movie*****

Title: Ishtar

Type: Comedy

Format: VHS

Rating: PG

Description: Viewable boredom

PYTHON PROGRAMS

Python Program to Add Two Matrices

```
# Program to add two matrices
# using nested loop
X = [[12,7,3],
    [4 ,5,6],
    [7 ,8,9]]

Y = [[5,8,1],
    [6,7,3],
    [4,5,9]]
```

```
result = [[0,0,0],
         [0,0,0],
         [0,0,0]]
# iterate through rows
for i in range(len(X)):
   # iterate through columns
   for j in range(len(X[0])):
       result[i][j] = X[i][j] + Y[i][j]
for r in result:
   print(r)
```

Output:

```
[17, 15, 4]
[10, 12, 9]
[11, 13, 18]
```

Python Program to Add Two Numbers

```
# This program adds two numbers

# Numbers are provided by the user

# Store input numbers

num1 = input('Enter first number: ')

num2 = input('Enter second number: ')

# Add two numbers

sum = float(num1) + float(num2)

# Display the sum

print('The sum of {0} and {1} is
{2}'.format(num1,num2,sum))
```

Output:

```
Enter first number: 5.3
```

```
Enter second number: 3.3

The sum of 5.3 and 3.3 is 8.6
```

Python Program to Calculate the Area of a Triangle

```
# Python Program to find the area of triangle

# Three sides of the triangle

# a,b,c are provided by the user

a = float(input('Enter first side: '))

b = float(input('Enter second side: '))

c = float(input('Enter third side: '))

# calculate the semi-perimeter

s = (a + b + c) / 2
```

```
# calculate the area

area = (s*(s-a)*(s-b)*(s-c)) ** 0.5

print('The area of the triangle is %0.2f'
%area)
```

Output:

```
Enter first side: 5

Enter second side: 6

Enter third side: 7

The area of the triangle is 14.70
```

Python Program to Check Armstrong Number

```
# Python program to if the

# number provided by the
```

```
# user is an Armstrong number

# or not

# take input from the user

num = int(input("Enter a number: "))

# initialise sum

sum = 0

# find the sum of the cube of each digit

temp = num

while temp > 0:

  digit = temp % 10

  sum += digit ** 3

  temp //= 10

# display the result

if num == sum:

  print(num,"is an Armstrong number")
```

```
else:
   print(num,"is not an Armstrong number")
```

Output 1

```
Enter a number: 663
663 is not an Armstrong number
```

Output 2

```
Enter a number: 371
407 is an Armstrong number
```

Python Program to Check if a Number is Odd or Even

```
# Python program to check if
```

```
# the input number is odd or even.
# A number is even if division
# by 2 give a remainder of 0.
# If remainder is 1, it is odd.
num = int(input("Enter a number: "))
if (num % 2) == 0:
  print("{0} is Even".format(num))
else:
  print("{0} is Odd".format(num))
```

Output 1

```
Enter a number: 73
73 is Odd
```

Output 2

```
Enter a number: 24

24 is Even
```

Python Program to Check if a Number is Positive, Negative or Zero

```
# In this python program, we input a
number

# check if the number is positive or

# negative or zero and display

# an appropriate message

num = float(input("Enter a number: "))

if num > 0:

   print("Positive number")
```

```
elif num == 0:
    print("Zero")
else:
    print("Negative number")
# In this program, we input a number
# check if the number is positive or
# negative or zero and display
# an appropriate message
# This time we use nested if
num = float(input("Enter a number: "))
if num >= 0:
    if num == 0:
        print("Zero")
    else:
        print("Positive number")
```

```
else:
  print("Negative number")
```

Output 1

```
Enter a number: 5
Positive number
```

Output 2

```
Enter a number: 0
Zero
```

Output 3

```
Enter a number: -4
Negative number
```

Python Program to Check if a String is Palindrome or Not

```
# Program to check if a string

#  is palindrome or not

# take input from the user

my_str = input("Enter a string: ")

# make it suitable for caseless comparison

my_str = my_str.casefold()

# reverse the string

rev_str = reversed(my_str)

# check if the string is equal to its reverse

if list(my_str) == list(rev_str):

  print("It is palindrome")

else:

  print("It is not palindrome")
```

Output 1

Enter a string: albohPhoBiA

It is palindrome

Output 2

Enter a string: 13344331

It is palindrome

Output 3

Enter a string: palindrome

It is not palindrome

Python Program to Check Leap Year

```
# Python program to check if
```

```
# the input year is
# a leap year or not
year = int(input("Enter a year: "))
if (year % 4) == 0:
  if (year % 100) == 0:
    if (year % 400) == 0:
      print("{0} is a leap year".format(year))
    else:
      print("{0} is not a leap
year".format(year))
  else:
    print("{0} is a leap year".format(year))
else:
  print("{0} is not a leap year".format(year))
```

Output 1

```
Enter a year: 2012

2012 is a leap year
```

Output 2

```
Enter a year: 2015

2015 is not a leap year
```

Python Program to Check Prime Number

```
# Python program to check if

# the input number is

# prime or not

# take input from the user
```

```
num = int(input("Enter a number: "))
# prime numbers are greater than 1
if num > 1:
  # check for factors
  for i in range(2,num):
     if (num % i) == 0:
        print(num,"is not a prime number")
        print(i,"times",num//i,"is",num)
        break
  else:
     print(num,"is a prime number")
# if input number is less than
# or equal to 1, it is not prime
else:
  print(num,"is not a prime number")
```

Output 1

Enter a number: 407

407 is not a prime number

11 times 37 is 407

Output 2

Enter a number: 853

853 is a prime number

Python Program to Convert Celsius To Fahrenheit

```
# Python Program to convert temperature in
# celsius to fahrenheit where, input is
# provided by the user in
```

```
# degree celsius

# take input from the user

celsius = float(input('Enter degree Celsius: '))

# calculate fahrenheit

fahrenheit = (celsius * 1.8) + 32

print('%0.1f degree Celsius is equal to %0.1f degree Fahrenheit' %(celsius,fahrenheit))
```

Output

```
Enter degree Celsius: 43.7

43.7 degree Celsius is equal to 110.66 degree Fahrenheit
```

Python Program to Convert Decimal into Binary, Octal and Hexadecimal

```
# Python program to convert decimal
# number into binary, octal and
# hexadecimal number system
# Take decimal number from user
dec = int(input("Enter an integer: "))
print("The decimal value of",dec,"is:")
print(bin(dec),"in binary.")
print(oct(dec),"in octal.")
print(hex(dec),"in hexadecimal.")
```

Output

```
Enter an integer: 133
The decimal value of 133 is:
```

0b10000101 in binary.

0o205 in octal.

0x85 in hexadecimal.

Python Program to Convert Decimal to Binary Using Recursion

```
# Python program to convert decimal
# number into binary number
# using recursive function
def binary(n):
  """Function to print binary number
  for the input decimal using recursion"""
  if n > 1:
     binary(n//2)
```

```
 print(n % 2,end = '')
# Take decimal number from user
dec = int(input("Enter an integer: "))
binary(dec)
```

Output

```
Enter an integer: 76
1001100
```

Python Program to Convert Kilometers to Miles

```
# Program to convert kilometers
# into miles where, input is
# provided by the user in
```

```
# kilometers

# take input from the user

kilometers = float(input('How many
kilometers?: '))

# conversion factor

conv_fac = 0.621371

# calculate miles

miles = kilometers * conv_fac

print('%0.3f kilometers is equal to %0.3f
miles' %(kilometers,miles))
```

Output

```
How many kilometers?: 3.7

5.500 kilometers is equal to 2.300 miles
```

Python Program to Count the Number of Each Vowel

```
# Program to count the number of

# each vowel in a string

# string of vowels

vowels = 'aeiou'

# take input from the user

ip_str = input("Enter a string: ")

# make it suitable for caseless comparisions

ip_str = ip_str.casefold()

# make a dictionary with each vowel a key
and value 0

count = {}.fromkeys(vowels,0)

# count the vowels

for char in ip_str:
```

```
  if char in count:
     count[char] += 1
print(count)
```

Output

Enter a string: I welcome you all to read my book and learn python easily.

{'e': 4, 'u': 1, 'o': 6, 'a': 5, 'i': 1}

Python Program to Display Calendar

```
# Python program to display calendar
# of given month of the year
# import module
import calendar
```

```
# ask of month and year

yy = int(input("Enter year: "))

mm = int(input("Enter month: "))

# display the calendar

print(calendar.month(yy,mm))
```

Output

```
Enter year: 2015

Enter month: 09

   September 2015

Mo  Tu  We  Th  Fr  Sa  Su
     1   2   3   4   5   6
 7   8   9  10  11  12  13
14  15  16  17  18  19  20
21  22  23  24  25  26  27
28  29  30
```

Python Program to Display Fibonacci Sequence Using Recursion

```
# Python program to display the Fibonacci
# sequence up to n-th term using
# recursive functions
def recur_fibo(n):
  """Recursive function to
  print Fibonacci sequence"""
  if n <= 1:
     return n
  else:
     return(recur_fibo(n-1) + recur_fibo(n-
2))
# take input from the user
nterms = int(input("How many terms? "))
```

```
# check if the number of terms is valid
if nterms <= 0:
  print("Plese enter a positive integer")
else:
  print("Fibonacci sequence:")
  for i in range(nterms):
      print(recur_fibo(i))
```

Output

```
How many terms? 8
Fibonacci sequence:
0
1
1
2
```

```
3

5

8

13
```

Python Program To Display Powers of 2 Using Anonymous Function

```
# Python Program to display

# the powers of 2 using

# anonymous function

# Take number of terms from user

terms = int(input("How many terms? "))

# use anonymous function
```

```
result = list(map(lambda x: 2 ** x,
range(terms)))

# display the result

for i in range(terms):

   print("2 raised to power",i,"is",result[i])
```

Output

```
How many terms? 6

2 raised to power 0 is 1

2 raised to power 1 is 2

2 raised to power 2 is 4

2 raised to power 3 is 8

2 raised to power 4 is 16

2 raised to power 5 is 32
```

Python Program to Display the multiplication Table

```
# Python program to find the multiplication

# table (from 1 to 10)c

# of a number input by the user

# take input from the user

num = int(input("Display multiplication table of? "))

# use for loop to iterate 10 times

for i in range(1,11):

   print(num,'x',i,'=',num*i)
```

Output

```
Display multiplication table of? 7

7 x 1 = 7
```

```
7 x 2 = 14

7 x 3 = 21

7 x 4 = 28

7 x 5 = 35

7 x 6 = 42

7 x 7 = 49

7 x 8 = 56

7 x 9 = 63

7 x 10 = 70
```

Python Program to Find Armstrong Number in an Interval

```
# Program to ask the user

# for a range and display
```

```
# all Armstrong numbers in
# that interval
# take input from the user
lower = int(input("Enter lower range: "))
upper = int(input("Enter upper range: "))
for num in range(lower,upper + 1):
  # initialize sum
  sum = 0
  # find the sum of the cube of each digit
  temp = num
  while temp > 0:
     digit = temp % 10
     sum += digit ** 3
     temp //= 10
  if num == sum:
```

```
print(num)
```

Output

```
Enter lower range: 0

Enter upper range: 999

0

1

153

370

371

407
```

Python Program to Find ASCII Value of Character

```
# Program to find the

# ASCII value of the

# given character

# Take character from user

c = input("Enter a character: ")

print("The ASCII value of '" + c + "' is",ord(c))
```

Output 1

```
Enter a character: k

The ASCII value of 'k' is 107
```

Output 2

```
Enter a character: =

The ASCII value of '=' is 61
```

Python Program to Find Factorial of Number Using Recursion

```
# Python program to find the
# factorial of a number
# using recursion
def recur_factorial(n):
  """Function to return the factorial
  of a number using recursion"""
  if n == 1:
     return n
  else:
     return n*recur_factorial(n-1)
# take input from the user
num = int(input("Enter a number: "))
# check is the number is negative
```

```
if num < 0:
   print("Sorry, factorial does not exist for negative numbers")
elif num == 0:
   print("The factorial of 0 is 1")
else:
   print("The factorial of",num,"is",recur_factorial(num))
```

Output 1

Enter a number: -5

Sorry, factorial does not exist for negative numbers

Output 2

Enter a number: 5

The factorial of 5 is 120

Python Program to Find Factors of Number

```
# Python Program to find the
# factors of a number
# define a function
def print_factors(x):
  """This function takes a
  number and prints the factors"""
  print("The factors of",x,"are:")
  for i in range(1, x + 1):
      if x % i == 0:
          print(i)
# take input from the user
num = int(input("Enter a number: "))
print_factors(num)
```

Output

Enter a number: 120

The factors of 120 are:

1

2

3

4

5

6

8

10

12

15

20

24

```
30
40
60
120
```

Python Program to Find Hash of File

```
# Python rogram to find the SHA-1
# message digest of a file
# import hashlib module
import hashlib
def hash_file(filename):
   """"This function returns the SHA-1 hash
   of the file passed into it"""
```

```
    # make a hash object
    h = hashlib.sha1()
    # open file for reading in binary mode
    with open(filename,'rb') as file:
        # loop till the end of the file
        chunk = 0
        while chunk != b'':
            # read only 1024 bytes at a time
            chunk = file.read(1024)
            h.update(chunk)
    # return the hex representation of digest
    return h.hexdigest()
message = hash_file("track1.mp3")
print(message)
```

Output

```
633d7356947eec543c50b76a1852f92427f4
dca9
```

Python Program to Find HCF or GCD

```
# Python program to find the
# H.C.F of two input number
# define a function
def hcf(x, y):
   """This function takes two
   integers and returns the H.C.F"""
   # choose the smaller number
   if x > y:
       smaller = y
```

```
    else:
        smaller = x
    for i in range(1,smaller + 1):
        if((x % i == 0) and (y % i == 0)):
            hcf = i
   return
# take input from the user
num1 = int(input("Enter first number: "))
num2 = int(input("Enter second number: "))
print("The H.C.F. of", num1,"and",
num2,"is", hcf(num1, num2))
```

Output

```
Enter first number: 40
Enter second number: 48
The H.C.F. of 40 and 48 is 8
```

Python Program to Find LCM

```
# Python Program to find the
# L.C.M. of two input number
# define a function
def lcm(x, y):
   """This function takes two
   integers and returns the L.C.M."""
   # choose the greater number
   if x > y:
       greater = x
   else:
       greater = y
   while(True):
       if((greater % x == 0) and (greater % y ==
0)):
```

```
        lcm = greater
        break
      greater += 1
   return lcm
# take input from the user
num1 = int(input("Enter first number: "))
num2 = int(input("Enter second number: "))
print("The L.C.M. of", num1,"and",
num2,"is", lcm(num1, num2))
```

Output

```
Enter first number: 3
Enter second number: 4
The L.C.M. of 3 and 4 is 12
```

Python Program to Find Numbers Divisible by Another Number

```
# Python Program to find numbers

# divisible by thirteen

# from a list using anonymous function

# Take a list of numbers

my_list = [12, 65, 54, 39, 102, 339, 221,]

# use anonymous function to filter

result = list(filter(lambda x: (x % 13 == 0),
my_list))

# display the result

print("Numbers divisible by 13 are",result)
```

Output

```
Numbers divisible by 13 are [65, 39, 221]
```

Python Program to Find Sum of Natural Numbers Using Recursion

```
# Python program to find the sum of
# natural numbers up to n
# using recursive function
def recur_sum(n):
   """Function to return the sum
   of natural numbers using recursion"""
   if n <= 1:
       return n
   else:
       return n + recur_sum(n-1)
# take input from the user
num = int(input("Enter a number: "))
if num < 0:
```

```
  print("Enter a positive number")
else:
  print("The sum is",recur_sum(num))
```

Output

```
Enter a number: 10
The sum is 55
```

Python Program to Find the Factorial of a Number

```
# Python program to find the
# factorial of a number
# provided by the user
```

```
# take input from the user

num = int(input("Enter a number: "))

factorial = 1

# check if the number is negative, positive
or zero

if num < 0:

  print("Sorry, factorial does not exist for
negative numbers")

elif num == 0:

  print("The factorial of 0 is 1")

else:

  for i in range(1,num + 1):

     factorial = factorial*i

  print("The factorial of",num,"is",factorial)
```

Output 1

Enter a number: -18

Sorry, factorial does not exist for negative numbers

Output 2

Enter a number: 9

The factorial of 9 is 362,880

Python Program to Find the Largest Among Three Numbers

```
# Python program to find the largest

# number among the three

# input numbers
```

```
# take three numbers from user

num1 = float(input("Enter first number: "))

num2 = float(input("Enter second number:
"))

num3 = float(input("Enter third number: "))

if (num1 > num2) and (num1 > num3):

  largest = num1

elif (num2 > num1) and (num2 > num3):

  largest = num2

else:

  largest = num3

print("The largest number is",largest)
```

Output 1

```
Enter first number: 8

Enter second number: 16
```

```
Enter third number: 4

The largest number is 16.0
```

Output 2

```
Enter first number: -6

Enter second number: -15

Enter third number: 0

The largest number is 0.0
```

Python Program to Find the Size (Resolution) of Image

```
# Python Program to find the resolution

# of a jpeg image without using
```

```
# any external libraries

def jpeg_res(filename):

  """"This function prints the resolution

  of the jpeg image file passed into it""""

  # open image for reading in binary mode

  with open(filename,'rb') as img_file:

     # height of image (in 2 bytes) is at 164th
position

     img_file.seek(163)

     # read the 2 bytes

     a = img_file.read(2)

     # calculate height

     height = (a[0] << 8) + a[1]

     # next 2 bytes is width

     a = img_file.read(2)

     # calculate width
```

```
    width = (a[0] << 8) + a[1]

  print("The resolution of the image is",width,"x",height)

jpeg_res("image.jpg")
```

Output

```
The resolution of the image is 180 x 200
```

Python Program to Find the Square Root

```
# Python Program to calculate the square root

num = float(input('Enter a number: '))

num_sqrt = num ** 0.5
```

```
print('The square root of %0.3f is
%0.3f'%(num ,num_sqrt))
```

Output

```
Enter a number: 11

The square root of 11.000 is 3.316
```

Python Program to Find the Sum of Natural Numbers

```
# Python program to find the sum of

# natural numbers up to n

# where n is provided by user

# take input from the user
```

```
num = int(input("Enter a number: "))
if num < 0:
   print("Enter a positive number")
else:
   sum = 0
   # use while loop to iterate un till zero
   while(num > 0):
       sum += num
       num -= 1
   print("The sum is",sum)
```

Output

```
Enter a number: 10
The sum is 55
```

Python Program to Generate a Random Number

```
# Program to generate a random number

# between 0 and 9

# import the random module

import random

print(random.randint(0,9))
```

Output

```
5
```

Python Program to Illustrate Different Set Operations

```
# Program to perform different
```

```
# set operations like in mathematics

# define three sets

E = {0, 2, 4, 6, 8};

N = {1, 2, 3, 4, 5};

# set union

print("Union of E and N is",E | N)

# set intersection

print("Intersection of E and N is",E & N)

# set difference

print("Difference of E and N is",E - N)

# set symmetric difference

print("Symmetric difference of E and N is",E
^ N)
```

Output

```
Union of E and N is {0, 1, 2, 3, 4, 5, 6, 8}
```

Intersection of E and N is {2, 4}

Difference of E and N is {8, 0, 6}

Symmetric difference of E and N is {0, 1, 3, 5, 6, 8}

Python Program to Make a Simple Calculator

```
# Program make a simple calculator

# that can add, subtract, multiply

# and divide using functions

# define functions

def add(x, y):

   """This function adds two numbers"""
```

```
  return x + y
def subtract(x, y):
  """This function subtracts two numbers"""
  return x - y
def multiply(x, y):
  """This function multiplies two
numbers"""
  return x * y
def divide(x, y):
  """This function divides two numbers"""
  return x / y
# take input from the user
print("Select operation.")
print("1.Add")
print("2.Subtract")
print("3.Multiply")
```

```
print("4.Divide")

choice = input("Enter choice(1/2/3/4):")

num1 = int(input("Enter first number: "))

num2 = int(input("Enter second number: "))

if choice == '1':

  print(num1,"+",num2,"=",
add(num1,num2))

elif choice == '2':

  print(num1,"-",num2,"=",
subtract(num1,num2))

elif choice == '3':

  print(num1,"*",num2,"=",
multiply(num1,num2))

elif choice == '4':

  print(num1,"/",num2,"=",
divide(num1,num2))

else:
```

```
print("Invalid input")
```

Output

```
Select operation.
1.Add
2.Subtract
3.Multiply
4.Divide
Enter choice(1/2/3/4): 2
Enter first number: 20
Enter second number: 11
20 - 11 = 9
```

Python Program to Multiply Two Matrices

```
# Program to multiply two matrices

# using nested loops

# 3x3 matrix

X = [[12,7,3],

   [4 ,5,6],

   [7 ,8,9]]

# 3x4 matrix


Y = [[5,8,1,2],

   [6,7,3,0],

   [4,5,9,1]]

# result is 3x4

result = [[0,0,0,0],
```

```
         [0,0,0,0],
         [0,0,0,0]]
# iterate through rows of X
for i in range(len(X)):
   # iterate through columns of Y
   for j in range(len(Y[0])):
       # iterate through rows of Y
       for k in range(len(Y)):
           result[i][j] += X[i][k] * Y[k][j]
for r in result:
   print(r)
```

Output

```
[114, 160, 60, 27]
[74, 97, 73, 14]
[119, 157, 112, 23]
```

Python Program to Print all Prime Numbers in an Interval

```
# Python program to ask the user

# for a range and display

# all the prime numbers in

# that interval

# take input from the user

lower = int(input("Enter lower range: "))

upper = int(input("Enter upper range: "))

for num in range(lower,upper + 1):

  # prime numbers are greater than 1

  if num > 1:

     for i in range(2,num):

        if (num % i) == 0:

           break
```

```
    else:
        print(num)
```

Output

```
Enter lower range: 100
Enter upper range: 200
101
103
107
109
113
127
131
137
139
```

149

151

157

163

167

173

179

181

191

193

197

199

Python Program to Print Hi Good Morning!

```
# This program prints Hi, Good Morning!

print('Hi, Good Morning!')
```

Output

```
Hi, Good Morning!
```

Python program to Print the Fibonacci sequence

```
# Program to display the fibonacci

# sequence up to n-th tern where

# n is provided by the user
```

```
# take input from the user

nterms = int(input("How many terms? "))

# first two terms

n1 = 0

n2 = 1

count = 2

# check if the number of terms is valid

if nterms <= 0:

  print("Plese enter a positive integer")

elif nterms == 1:

  print("Fibonacci sequence:")

  print(n1)

else:

  print("Fibonacci sequence:")

  print(n1,",",n2,end=' , ')
```

```
while count < nterms:
    nth = n1 + n2
    print(nth,end=' , ')
    # update values
    n1 = n2
    n2 = nth
    count += 1
```

Output

```
How many terms? 12
Fibonacci sequence:
0 , 1 , 1 , 2 , 3 , 5 , 8 , 13 , 21 , 34 , 55 , 89
```

Python Program to Remove Punctuations form a String

```
# Program to all punctuations from the
# string provided by the user
# define punctuations
punctuations = '''!()-
[]{};:'"\,<>./?@#$%^&*_~'''
# take input from the user
my_str = input("Enter a string: ")
# remove punctuations from the string
no_punct = ""
for char in my_str:
   if char not in punctuations:
      no_punct = no_punct + char
# display the unpunctuated string
```

```
print(no_punct)
```

Output

```
Enter a string: "Hello!!!", Good Morning ---
Have a good day.

Hello Good Morning Have a good day
```

Python Program to Shuffle Deck of Cards

```
# Python program to shuffle a

# deck of card using the

# module random and draw 5 cards

# import modules

import itertools, random
```

```
# make a deck of cards

deck =
list(itertools.product(range(1,14),['Spade','Heart','Diamond','Club']))

# shuffle the cards

random.shuffle(deck)

# draw five cards

print("You got:")

for i in range(5):

  print(deck[i][0], "of", deck[i][1])
```

Output 1

```
You got:

5 of Heart

1 of Heart

8 of Spade
```

12 of Spade

4 of Spade

Output 2

You got:

10 of Club

1 of Heart

3 of Diamond

2 of Club

3 of Club

Python Program to Solve Quadratic Equation

```
# Solve the quadratic equation

# ax**2 + bx + c = 0
```

```
# a,b,c are provied by the user

# import complex math module

import cmath

a = float(input('Enter a: '))

b = float(input('Enter b: '))

c = float(input('Enter c: '))

# calculate the discriminant

d = (b**2) - (4*a*c)

# find two solutions

sol1 = (-b-cmath.sqrt(d))/(2*a)

sol2 = (-b+cmath.sqrt(d))/(2*a)

print('The solution are {0} and
{1}'.format(sol1,sol2))
```

Output

```
Enter a: 1
```

```
Enter b: 5

Enter c: 6

The solutions are (-3+0j) and (-2+0j)
```

Python Program to Sort Words in Alphabetic Order

```
# Program to sort alphabetically the words

# form a string provided by the user

# take input from the user

my_str = input("Enter a string: ")

# breakdown the string into a list of words

words = my_str.split()

# sort the list

words.sort()
```

```
# display the sorted words
for word in words:
   print(word)
```

Output

```
Enter a string: this is my second python
book to read
book
is
my
python
read
second
this
to
```

Python Program to Swap Two Variables

```
# Python program to swap two variables

# provided by the user

x = input('Enter value of x: ')

y = input('Enter value of y: ')

# create a temporary variable

# and swap the values

temp = x

x = y

y = temp

print('The value of x after swapping:
{}'.format(x))

print('The value of y after swapping:
{}'.format(y))
```

Output

```
Enter value of x: 8

Enter value of y: 15

The value of x after swapping: 15

The value of y after swapping: 8
```

Python Program to Transpose a Matrix

```
# Program to transpose a matrix

# using nested loop

X = [[12,7],

   [4 ,5],

   [3 ,8]]
```

```
result = [[0,0,0],
        [0,0,0]]


# iterate through rows
for i in range(len(X)):
  # iterate through columns
  for j in range(len(X[0])):
      result[j][i] = X[i][j]
for r in result:
  print(r)
```

Output

```
[12, 4, 3]
[7, 5, 8]
```

NOTE

This is all about Python Programming. These things are must to understand if you are a beginner in learning Python Program Language. I Hope you liked the book and learned a lot from it. The book is a Quick & Easy Guide To Learn Python Programming Language. This book includes functions, classes, databases used in python. The book also includes various python programs that will be very helpful for you to create your own programs. You can become a good python programmer by going through this book. Also it has examples and syntax included in it. With this book you can learn professional Python style, best practices, and good programming habits. You can also improve application performance by writing extensions using multithreading. You can become a good python programmer by going through this book. Book also contains basic programs written in python. There are around 50 programs you will find in this book. I have also shared basic python programs in this book, so what are you waiting for?? Turn on your system and start creating your Python Programs.

DISCLAIMER

This eBook gives the reader an insight on python programming language. It is an original eBook with no content copied from any site or book. Therefore, the owner should be contacted if any contents in this book are needed to be used in other books or websites.

The materials written in this eBook are unique to this site. The site makes no warranties, uttered, and, therefore, disowns and cancels all other warranties, as well as without restraint, indirect warranties or circumstances of merchantability, or other infringement of rights.

Also, this site does not call for or make any illustrations regarding the precision, probable results, or dependability of the utilization of the materials on this site or if not connecting to such materials or on any websites connected to this website.

MORE FROM AUTHOR

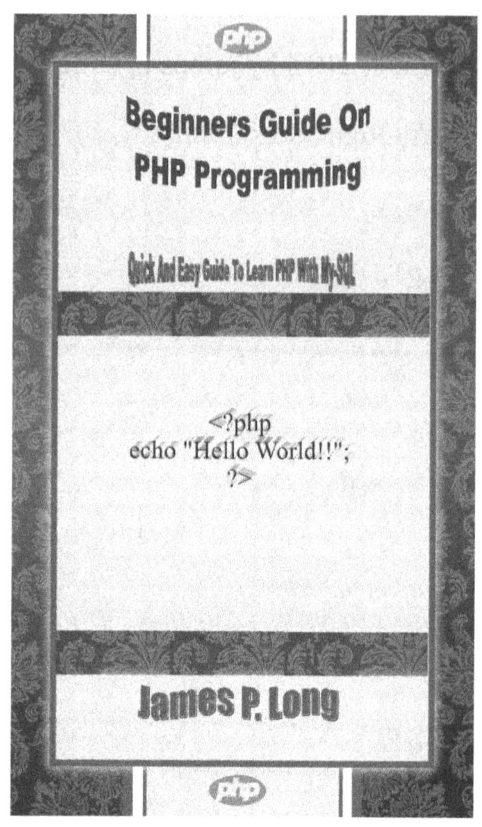

Beginners Guide On PHP Programming: Quick And Easy Guide To Learn PHP With My-SQL

The Book - Beginners Guide On PHP Programming is written by James P. Long. This book includes all the basics of PHP, functions, classes, objects, databases used in PHP programming. With this book you can learn professional PHP style, best practices, MY-SQL databases, HTML Forms, PHP graphics and good programming habits. You can become a good PHP programmer by going through this book.

ABOUT AUTHOR

Hi, I am James P. Long.

I'm a web developer who has been designing and developing websites professionally for so many years. I'm a fast learner and I have knowledge of different programming languages. I am so much passionate about programming. I have learned many programming languages very quickly and I want to teach it to others as well in a simple and easy way to understand.

I have vast knowledge on the best and fastest ways to learn Programming languages. I always like to teach and help people understand the most complex things in simpler things. So, I decided to write my own courses in the form of kindle books, where you can learn quickly and easily how to use programming languages such as Python, C, C++, etc.

My first book, which I have released was "Python Programming for Beginners", its series book, after that I launched its next series "Complete Guide For Python Programming", which has advanced functions and programs in it. There after python I wrote another book on PHP Programming, "Beginners Guide On PHP Programming". Soon I will share more programming languages with you. Till than enjoyed reading these books and follow me, to get recent updates... Thanks

www.ingramcontent.com/pod-product-compliance
Lightning Source LLC
Chambersburg PA
CBHW071357050326
40689CB00010B/1672

* 9 7 8 1 5 1 4 6 1 8 9 0 5 *